Farming Simulator Modding

FOR

DUMMIES®

A Wiley Brand

Farming Simulator Modding

FOR

DUMMIES®

A Wiley Brand

by Jason van Gumster

and

Christian Ammann

FOR

DUMMIES®

A Wiley Brand

Farming Simulator Modding For Dummies®

Published by
John Wiley & Sons, Inc.
111 River St.
Hoboken, NJ 07030-5774
www.wiley.com

ISBN 978-1-118-94025-9

ISBN 978-1-118-94025-9 (pbk); ISBN 978-1-118-94028-0 (ebk);

Printed and bound in Great Britain by Bell & Bain Ltd, Glasgow

Manufactured in the United States of America

10 9 8 7 6 5 4 3 2

Table of Contents

Introduction

*Y*ou'll often hear two comments from nearly anyone who has played any version of Farming Simulator released in the last few years.

- ✔ **"I had no idea this game would be so addictive."**
  A person often gets the game on a lark, purchasing it from a favorite retail outlet or downloading it via Steam or www.farming-simulator.com. You then start playing. The next thing you know, hours have flown by and you're eyeballing a new fork for the front loader you just bought so you can move more bales around your steadily growing farm. It's not at all uncommon for a person to dump more than a 100 hours of gameplay into Farming Simulator within only a few weeks. Only then does it begin to sink in as to why this game has become so incredibly popular, with more than 5 million copies sold worldwide.

- ✔ **"I didn't realize how incredibly large and active the modding community is for this game."** *Mod* is short for *modification,* and GIANTS Software has made it incredibly easy to make modifications to Farming Simulator and share those mods with others. If you want proof of how big modding is for this game, type "farming simulator mods" into your favorite search engine. On even a basic search, you can find more than a dozen different mod communities for Farming Simulator, each one with more than 1,000 unique mods. In fact, more than 15,000 mods have been created just for Farming Simulator 2013! You can find everything from a simple ramp or new tractor to custom maps and reconfigured game mechanics. There's even a mod that turns Farming Simulator into a flight simulator! And the community creates more mods each and every day. There's something incredibly rewarding about making your own custom *thing* for a game — taking ownership of it, if you will — and then actually using it in the game environment with others.

So Farming Simulator is not only a lot of fun to play, but it's also equally fun to customize.

About This Book

Farming Simulator Modding For Dummies serves as a reference for each step in the process of making mods. That process is simultaneously artistic and technical, spanning a wide array of tools and disciplines. For this reason, you often see people group together and form mod teams, so individuals with a more specialized skill can focus on what they're good at. If you're making the full mod yourself, this book can help guide you through it. If you're one person on a team, the book covers your specialization while also giving you an understanding of what the other members of your team need (as well as what you should expect from them).

This book isn't large enough to be comprehensive, so I focus on just what you need to know to start building mods. Some subjects simply are out of scope. For example, on the art side, I cover polygon budgets for models and the process of getting your 3D models properly optimized for the Farming Simulator engine, but there isn't enough room to cover 3D modeling as a topic. (That would be a book by itself!) Likewise, on the technical side, I can show you the structure of the modDesc.xml file and introduce the possibilities in customizing your mod with Lua, but you'll need to look online for the full API.

All the screenshots were taken on a computer running the Windows operating system. Although Farming Simulator *does* run on Mac OS X, most of the modding community uses Windows. Generally, there aren't too many differences, but I make note of where they do crop up. On a related note, if you're using a Mac and only have a trackpad, I can't emphasize enough the value in working with a proper three-button mouse. Most applications that work in 3D, including the ones covered in this book, expect you to have one. If you're adept at using the trackpad and gestures to simulate a three-button mouse, you may be fine, but advanced gestures like pinching and rotating aren't likely to work for you.

Also, when it comes to creating 3D content for your mods, you can use a wide variety of tools. This book references the three most common ones used in the Farming Simulator modding community: Blender, Maya, and 3ds Max. Because it's free (and because it's my personal favorite), most of the references in this book focus on Blender. When something is specific to Maya or 3ds Max, I point it out.

As I discuss various software programs in this book, I tell you how to find an operation in a menu using this symbol: ⇨, such as "Go to File⇨Open to open a file." That said, regardless of the program, I have a preference for using hotkeys because they're much faster. So where possible, I lead with the hotkey combination and include the menu navigation in parentheses. For example, "Open the file by pressing Ctrl+O (or File⇨Open in the menu)."

Foolish Assumptions

I assert a few assumptions about you in this book. In list form:

✔ **You have a computer capable of running Farming Simulator and GIANTS Editor.** It's pretty difficult to know if your mod works if you can't play the game. The system requirements for these are pretty modest; please refer to the manual for specifics.

✔ **You have a basic understanding of 3D graphics.** You don't need to be a professional video game programmer. If you know how to navigate in a 3D game and select things, that should be enough to get you started.

✔ **You're comfortable editing text files.** A lot of modding involves making adjustments to text files using a program like Notepad++. You *can* write them from scratch, but to start, you just need to know how to open them, make changes, and save.

I also assume that you can access the Internet from time to time. You don't need an Internet connection to make your mod, but a number of useful online resources are available, and you definitely need the Internet if you want to share your mod with others.

Beyond This Book

As this book is intended to give you a good, solid start in making mods for Farming Simulator, additional resources of information are available at your fingertips. Chapter 15 has a slew of these resources listed. However, other modders are the greatest source of information. The official forums on the GIANTS Developer Network (http://gdn. giants-software.com) and the Farming Simulator website (http://forum.giants-software.com) are a great start, but look at mod groups and mod hosting sites that are local to you as well. They're fountains of information as well as people willing to help.

Icons Used in This Book

These icons that appear in the book's margins can help you navigate your way through the book. Here is what they mean.

This icon calls out suggestions that help you work more effectively and save time.

Keep these useful pointers in mind as you produce your mods. Generally, you'll regularly encounter these things as you're working.

These icons point out moments that can get you pulling out your hair in frustration if you get caught in one.

Where to Go from Here

I am tempted to say, "To the fields!" Of course, you're making modifications for a game that simulates farming, so perhaps a bit of silliness is to be expected. If you're new to modding, then it makes the most sense to start at the beginning and work forward sequentially from Chapter 1. If you're familiar with modding, but you want to get up to speed with the specifics of creating mods for Farming Simulator, peruse the Table of Contents and find the chapter(s) that most interest you and read what you need.

Now, to the fields!

Part I
Getting Started with Farming Simulator Modding

getting started
with

Farming Simulator
Modding

In this part . . .

✔ Discover what modding is and the different ways that you can make changes in Farming Simulator

✔ Understand the fundamental tools used for modding Farming Simulator so you can begin creating your own mods

✔ Create map mods with your own custom terrain and foliage around buildings and other props as you see fit

✔ Familiarize yourself with how to control surface materials in Farming Simulator's 3D world

✔ Get a taste for how particles are used in a mod to bring life and realism to the game

Chapter 1

Introducing GIANTS Editor

● ●

In This Chapter

▶ Understanding the GIANTS Editor interface

▶ Opening 3D objects and scenes in the editor

▶ Moving around within a 3D scene in GIANTS Editor

▶ Moving, rotating, and scaling objects

● ●

*A*ll modding for Farming Simulator starts and ends with GIANTS Editor. If you want to make a quick change to a map or a vehicle, you can open its file and edit attributes in GIANTS Editor. If you've created a full mod from scratch, you pull all the pieces together and prepare them for inclusion in the game in GIANTS Editor. Think of GIANTS Editor as your modding dashboard.

You don't need to do a lot in order start working with GIANTS Editor; it ships with Farming Simulator. So if you've been playing the game, you're good to go with the editor; you just need to install it. You can find the install file in the sdk folder wherever you've installed Farming Simulator on your hard drive. (On a Windows computer, it's usually something like C:\Program Files (x86)\ Farming Simulator 2015.) Of course, going to the

GIANTS Developer Network website (http://gdn.
giants-software.com) and checking for updates is
still a good idea. That way you can be sure you get the
latest features and bug fixes. Updated versions of the
editor are free to download after you've registered on the
site (which is also free).

This chapter serves as your jumping-off point into the
world of creating mods for Farming Simulator by making
sure you have firm footing when it comes to using GIANTS
Editor. Regardless of how simple or complex your mod
may be, it needs to come through GIANTS Editor, so this
chapter is relevant, no matter your general modding
experience.

Knowing the Editor's Parts

When you first launch GIANTS Editor, you'll see a Getting
Started splash window that provides you with a hotkey
reference and a set of buttons that links you to a number of
useful resources to help quickly get you on the road to modding. You can toggle whether this window appears every
time you launch it by clicking the Show at startup checkbox in the window's lower-left corner. These resources
are certainly valuable, but you also have this book, so you
can comfortably close this window for the time being. You
can always bring it back from the Help menu in the editor
(Help⇨Getting Started . . .).

After you move past the splash window and actually
get into the editor, you may think it looks rather stark,
consisting of a set of mostly empty panels. Not to worry,
though, those panels will fill up pretty quickly. Figure 1-1
shows GIANTS Editor with the default interface and a
scene already loaded.

Figure 1-1: The GIANTS Editor default interface.

You can see four main panels when you first load GIANTS Editor:

✔ **Scenegraph:** You can find the Scenegraph on the far left of the editor window. The Scenegraph gives you a hierarchical view of the 3D scene, including all models, lights, and cameras. Think of it as an outline for your mod. In complex scenes, the Scenegraph panel is incredibly useful for selecting the object you're interested in editing.

✔ **3D Viewport:** The 3D Viewport is the large panel at the center of the editor window and is where the majority of your work takes place. Here you can select and manipulate objects in your mod; the 3D Viewport also provides a decent preview of what you can expect your mod to look like after you load it into Farming Simulator.

✔ **Attributes:** The Attributes panel on the far right of the editor window can show different settings and parameters, depending on the object you currently have selected. At the very least, any object you select will have Transform attributes for controlling how that object is positioned and oriented in 3D space. From there, depending on what the object is and what it does, it may have a wide variety of potential other subtabs available in the attributes panel. For example, in Figure 1-1, the selected building in that scene has a separate tab labeled LOD, for *level of detail*.

✔ **Scripting:** The Scripting panel is across the bottom of the editor window. This panel gives you a log and basic feedback on what's been done in your scene, such as loading external textures. It can also give you warnings if you have missing assets or if you've formatted something incorrectly in your mod. When things go pear-shaped in your mod, the Scripting panel is your best friend for troubleshooting what happened. And, of course, you can use the Scripting panel to type commands and make large automated changes to objects in your scene. Chapter 12 discusses scripting in greater depth.

With the exception of the 3D Viewport, you can move around any panel in the GIANTS Editor interface by clicking and dragging the panel's header bar. Doing so allows you to place the panel in another location or leave it as its own floating window. Being able to customize your interface is especially useful if you're working on a computer with multiple monitors. You can keep the 3D Viewport as big as possible on one monitor and move the other panels to your other monitor. Also, you can close any panel by clicking the little X on the right of the panel's header. You can bring back any closed panels from the Window menu.

Loading Assets

The file format that GIANTS Engine uses is the I3D format. I3D is an eXtensible Mark-up Language (XML) file format. That means, in part, that you can open it with a plain text editor and make changes to it. Chapters 6 and 11 discuss I3D and XML more.

For the purposes of this chapter, you just need to know that an I3D file encapsulates or references all the necessary data for a 3D asset in GIANTS Engine. That also means I3D files are what you load and modify from GIANTS Editor for your Farming Simulator mod. This section explains how to open full maps as well as individual assets that may appear on a map.

Opening an existing map

The easiest asset to open in GIANTS Editor is the default map that comes with Farming Simulator. Go to File⇨Open in GIANTS Editor and navigate to the maps folder within the folder where you've installed Farming Simulator (typically `C:\Program Files (x86)\Farming Simulator 2015\data\maps`) and choose the file named `map01.i3d`. You should see the familiar original map in the 3D Viewport after it finishes loading. Figure 1-2 shows the default Farming Simulator map loaded in GIANTS Editor.

Figure 1-2: The default Farming Simulator map (`map01.i3d`) opened within GIANTS Editor.

Do *not* save or overwrite the default Farming Simulator map, especially if you've made any changes to the file. At the very least, doing so may change the default behavior of the game. At worst, it may cause the game not to load and force you to reinstall it. Although Chapter 2 covers exporting the original map for modifications, right now your main focus should be on loading the map in GIANTS Editor and poking around to familiarize yourself with the interface.

Using this same basic method you can open any map scene. If you have any map mods installed, you can try opening up the map scenes from them as well.

Previewing objects

A Farming Simulator map is really a compilation of different 3D assets, including props, terrain, buildings, and so on. Suppose you're not interested in working with a full map, and you only want to have a look at one of the objects that appears on the map. You don't have to open the map in GIANTS Editor and hide everything except what you want to see.

You just need to follow the same basic steps for opening a map in GIANTS Editor. Find the I3D file for the object and open it from the editor. Figure 1-3 shows a mailbox from the default Farming Simulator map loaded in GIANTS Editor.

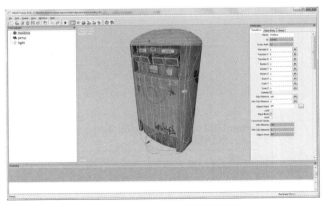

Figure 1-3: A mailbox object opened in GIANTS Editor.

When you first load an object in the editor, you may notice that the object may be really small in the 3D Viewport or out of view entirely. Fortunately, you can easily fix it with the following steps:

1. **If you can see the object in the 3D Viewport, you can select it by clicking on it.**

   If it's too small to select that way or if it's not visible in the 3D Viewport at all, you can click on the object's name in the Scenegraph panel and select it that way.

2. **With the object selected, you can frame the 3D Viewport on it using the F hotkey.**

   Doing so brings the object into view. However more than likely, the view will be too close to see the entire object. Using the scroll wheel on your mouse, you can back away from the object in the 3D Viewport and make it more visible. For more ways to navigate the 3D Viewport, refer to the next section.

You may also notice that your object appears really dark. Most objects don't emit light, so most object I3D files don't include any light in the scene, which can make previewing an object difficult.

To see the object clearly, you may want to add a light using the Ctrl+L hotkey combination. You can also add a light from the Create menu (Create⇨Light).

If you're viewing objects from the Farming Simulator data folder, *do not save* those object files, especially if you've made modifications like adding a light. Doing so affects how the object appears in the game.

Navigating in 3D Space

Being able to move around in the 3D Viewport to see the map or object from different angles is also important. You can move around by using the mouse and the Alt key on your keyboard.

Having a three-button mouse when working with 3D software is really in your best interest. These programs have a tendency to use as many buttons on your computer as they can get. Fortunately, most modern desktop computers come with three-button mice. (*Note:* You can find the third button on most of these mice by pressing down on the mouse's scroll wheel.) If you have a laptop, though, the built-in trackpad doesn't often have a middle mouse button. In that case, I highly recommend that you purchase a proper mouse.

Navigating a 3D scene consists of three main types of movement:

- **Orbiting:** The view from the 3D Viewport rotates around a fixed location. In GIANTS Editor, you orbit the view by holding Alt while clicking and dragging your left mouse button.

- **Panning:** The view from the 3D Viewport always faces the same direction, but it moves horizontally and vertically. Imagine that you're stepping side-to-side or squatting and standing while always looking the same direction. You pan in GIANTS Editor by holding Alt while clicking and dragging your middle mouse button.

- **Zooming:** The view from the 3D Viewport gets closer or farther away from a point in 3D space. A quick way to do this is with your mouse's scroll wheel. However, scrolling to zoom snaps in fixed increments. If you want more fine-grained control, hold Alt while clicking and dragging your right mouse button. Zooming this way is much smoother.

Using Framed Rotate

You can use another option for navigating in the 3D Viewport: Framed Rotate specifically relates to orbiting in the 3D Viewport. You can use the F hotkey to frame the 3D Viewport on the selected object. When you orbit the view with Framed Rotate enabled (View⇨Framed Rotate), you orbit around the last framed location, no matter how far away you pan from it.

Framed Rotate is great when you want to focus your attention on a single specific object. However, if you want to navigate a large scene like a map, having Framed Rotate enabled can make things difficult and unpredictable. When Framed Rotate is disabled, you can move about the 3D Viewport more freely. In fact, it feels a lot more like you're rotating the view camera while holding it rather than orbiting around a fixed point somewhere else in 3D space.

Choosing camera views

All I3D files have at least one camera object in them. The default camera is named *persp,* for *perspective.* However, some I3D files may have multiple cameras in the scene. These cameras are typically part of vehicle objects so the player has more than one option while driving. Of course, if you're interested in making a vehicle mod (or tweaking the camera angles in an existing vehicle), you need to see from the perspective of those cameras within GIANTS Editor.

You can change the current active camera from the View menu (View⇨Camera). This submenu has a list of every available camera in the I3D file. Clicking a camera's name in the menu automatically changes the 3D Viewport to see from that camera's perspective. Figure 1-4 shows the expanded View menu with the Camera submenu on a vehicle with two cameras.

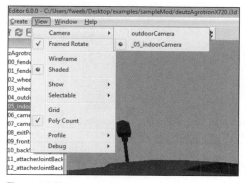

Figure 1-4: You can choose from two camera objects in this vehicle file.

Be careful about navigating in the 3D Viewport after changing to one of these vehicle cameras. By doing so, you're actually changing the position and orientation of the camera itself. For that reason, when opening a vehicle I3D file in GIANTS Editor, it's a good idea to add an additional camera to the scene to be your work camera. That way you don't mess up any of the vehicle's cameras. Of course, if you opened this file from Farming Simulator's data folder, you shouldn't be saving over it anyway. But creating a work camera is still a good practice to get into, just in case.

Transforming Objects

The real fun begins with modifying and changing things. Adjusting the location, rotation, or scale of an object in 3D space is called *transforming* the object. In GIANTS Editor, the easiest way to transform any active object is with the transform gizmo in the 3D Viewport. As shown in Figure 1-5, the transform gizmo looks like a 3D-axis surrounded by circles.

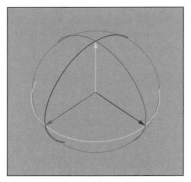

Figure 1-5: The transform gizmo allows you to move and rotate the active object.

The following sections examine the different ways that you can transform objects in GIANTS Editor.

Translating, rotating, and scaling

The transform gizmo gives you control over two types of transformations:

> ✔ **Translation:** Otherwise known as moving your object or changing its location. Use the gizmo to translate your active object by left-clicking and dragging one of the arrows on the gizmo's 3D axis.

> ✔ **Rotation:** To rotate your active object with the gizmo, left-click and drag along one of its three circles.

Another way that you can transform an active object is to scale or adjust its size. Unfortunately, the transform gizmo doesn't provide the facilities for adjusting scale. Instead, you need to make scaling adjustments from the Transform tab of the Attributes panel, as shown in Figure 1-6.

The translate, rotate, and scale fields take up the bulk of the space in the Transform tab of the Attributes panel. These text fields give you much more precise control over the location, orientation, and size of your active object. The following list gives additional information about each of these fields:

> ✔ **Translate X/Y/Z:** These values are measured in meters from the scene's origin (0m, 0m, 0m). Knowing the units here is especially important when putting an object on a map in a game. It can be pretty disorienting if you expect a part of a building to be 1cm off the ground, but it ends up floating 1m above the ground.

> ✔ **Rotate X/Y/Z:** These values are measured in degrees relative to the object's original rotation, which should be (0°, 0°, 0°).

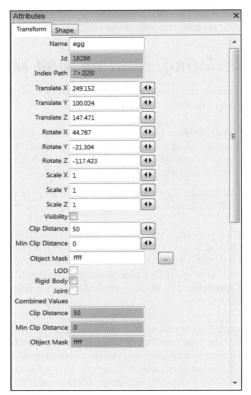

Figure 1-6: The Transform tab of the Attributes panel is available for any object in an I3D file.

✔ **Scale X/Y/Z:** These values are multiplied by the object's original scale, which should be (1, 1, 1). So if you set the scale values to (0.5, 0.5, 0.5), then it will be half of its original size. There isn't any way to lock the three scale values together, so if you want your object to be scaled uniformly, you need to double-check these values and make sure they're all the same.

In GIANTS Engine, the 3D environment is in a *y-up world*. That is, if you look at the 3D axis, the *y*-axis points up and down in the world, between the ground and the sky. Think of the plane defined by the *x*- and *z*-axis as the ground at sea level. The *x*-axis points east/west while the *z*-axis points north/south.

Selecting objects

You can also select multiple objects at once. The method that you use varies slightly depending on whether you're in the 3D Viewport or the Scenegraph.

- ✔ **3D Viewport:** You can add to the current selection set by Shift+left-clicking multiple objects. There is no way to remove an object from the current selection set, so if you select something incorrectly and you want to stay in the 3D Viewport, you'll need to redo your selection.

- ✔ **Scenegraph:** The Scenegraph is much better suited for multiple selection. You can toggle whether an object is part of the current selection set by Ctrl+left-clicking its name. Furthermore, if you click one object's name and Shift+left-click another name elsewhere on the tree, all of the objects between those two are also selected.

Regardless of how you make your multiple selection, the first object you select has a green wireframe whereas all additional selected objects have white wireframes. The green object is the *active object,* and its properties are the only ones editable from the Attributes panel. Furthermore, transformations with the transform gizmo in the 3D Viewport also only affect the active object. If you want to manipulate multiple objects at the same time, you need to make a new Transform Group and add those objects to it. Check out Chapter 2 for more information.

Chapter 2

Creating Map Mods

· ·

In This Chapter

▶ Setting up a map mod

▶ Adding props to your map

▶ Tweaking user attributes on the map

▶ Setting up event triggers at specific locations in a map

· ·

*M*aps are an excellent way to make mods and put something of your own in Farming Simulator. Farming Simulator comes with some great default maps, of course, but what if you want the ground to be hillier or you don't like the location of a particular building? Maybe you want to re-create your hometown and build a farm there. You can do all this and more, and it starts with making your own map mods.

This chapter examines how you can begin making maps for Farming Simulator, either by using default maps as a starting point or creating your own from scratch. Here you can also discover how to place props into your maps, make any adjustments to your maps after you've completed them, and establish event triggers in your maps to make them more interactive.

Preparing a Map Mod

Although the easiest way to get started with a map mod is to make changes to an existing map, just breaking open a map from the Farming Simulator installation folder and having at it isn't a great idea. Doing so would affect default gameplay on your computer and may cause the game not to work at all in multiplayer mode. More importantly, however, your newly modified map wouldn't be structured in a way that would be easy to share with other people who play Farming Simulator.

Here are the steps for making your own map mod in Farming Simulator.

1. **Create a new folder in the Farming Simulator `mods` folder.**

   You can do this on your desktop, but I prefer to make my folders right in Farming Simulator's mods folder, because that's ultimately where the map needs to end up if you want to play it. On Windows, you can find the mods folder in `Documents\MyGames\ FarmingSimulator2015\mods`.

   When naming the folder for your mod, keep in mind these simple rules:

   • You can't use spaces or special characters (such as @ or &) in the name.

   • You can't use numbers to start the name.

   So, for example, *myExcellentMap* is an acceptable folder name, whereas naming your folder *1stMap@theMoon* won't work when trying to load it in the game.

2. **Within your new custom folder for your mod, create a subfolder named `map`.**

3. **Start GIANTS Editor.**

   You can then build your own map from scratch. However, starting is much easier if you have some base elements in place. You may want your map mod to be based on the default map that ships with Farming Simulator.

4. Load an existing game map.

For example, C:\Program Files\Farming Simulator 2015\data\maps\map01.i3d.

5. Export the map to your custom folder by choosing File⇨Export All with Files from the menu.

When the file browser appears, navigate to the map folder within the custom mod folder you created (for instance, myExcellentMap), name the file map01.i3d, and click the Save button. The default map has quite a few assets included with it, so it might take a little while for the export process to complete, depending on how powerful your computer is.

Remember that you're exporting the map in this step. You're *not* saving it, regardless of what the button in the file browser says. Saving might make Farming Simulator unplayable in multiplayer with that map. Exporting doesn't have this potential effect.

6. After exporting, close GIANTS Editor.

If the editor prompts you to save, click No.

7. Extract Farming Simulator SDK to your custom mod folder.

The Farming Simulator SDK ships with the program. It's a Zip file in the sdk folder where Farming Simulator is installed (in Windows, look for something like C:\Program Files\Farming Simulator 2015\sdk\modMapSDK.zip).

To extract the Zip file (modMapSDK.zip) on a Windows computer, right-click the Zip file and choose Extract All. A dialog will ask where you want to extract the files. Click the Browse button in the dialog and navigate to the map folder you made within your mod's custom folder (for example, Documents\MyGames\FarmingSimulator2015\mods\myExcellentMap).

And that's it! Now you can begin editing your map mod.

Selecting, Organizing, and Placing Props

One of the fundamental aspects of map editing is selecting assets and moving them around the scene. These assets can include anything from lights and cameras to bushes and buildings. Although Chapter 1 covers the basics of selecting and transforming objects, the following sections explain how you can work more effectively with shortcuts for selecting groups of assets and placing them around your map, as well as importing external assets.

Making complex selections in the Scenegraph

In Chapter 1, I briefly cover your options for selecting assets in GIANTS Editor. To select assets, you can simply click on objects on the map. However, some objects in the scene are difficult to see, and others are only selectable after you drill down through their parent objects. This section covers using the Scenegraph to select exactly the assets in which you're interested.

When you make a selection in the 3D Viewport, look at the Scenegraph. Most objects are actually a group of assets hierarchically organized such that they're children of a parent object. The Scenegraph panel automatically updates and scrolls to your current selection. If your intent is to move or copy the whole object, you want to make sure that you select the parent. Doing so ensures that you also select all the child assets. In fact, you'll probably find yourself making selections in the Scenegraph at least as often as in the 3D Viewport.

Figure 2-1 shows the Scenegraph panel with an object selected (including all its children).

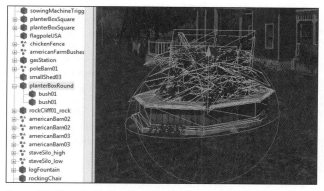

Figure 2-1: The *planterBoxRound* object is selected. The Scenegraph panel shows it has two children, both named *bush01*.

Because you're using the Scenegraph so often, make sure that your objects have clear, logical names that reflect what they are or what they do. You can easily get frustrated and confused if you find yourself making selections in a map where everything is named *mesh01* instead of *waterPump*, *oldBarn*, and *uglyTree*, for example.

Using interactive placement

Chapter 1 mentions that you can *transform* (move, rotate, or scale) your selection using the transform gizmo or by adjusting values in the Attributes panel. Although doing so works fine within a limited area with only a few objects, it can be tedious to work this way on even a modestly sized map. Fortunately, GIANTS Editor has a very convenient shortcut feature to help, called interactive placement.

Interactive placement allows you to take any selected object and place it on the surface of any other object in your map. To try it, make your selection and then press Ctrl+B (Edit⇨Interactive Placement in the menu). At this point, it's not obvious that anything has happened, but you're now in an interactive placement mode within the editor. If you left-click anywhere in your scene, your selected object *snaps,* or is placed on the surface you click. Even better, if you continue to hold down your left mouse button, you can interactively drag your object around. As you do so, your selection automatically snaps to the surface under your cursor. You can complete the move by releasing the left mouse button. Using this method, you can very quickly move an object from one part of your map to another.

If you don't want to move the object and instead you want to move a duplicate of it, don't worry. To duplicate, use the Ctrl+D hotkey combination (Edit⇨Duplicate). However, that's only useful on smaller mods. Map editing often involves duplicating and placing a several objects at a time. Fortunately, the interactive placement feature also integrates duplication.

To take advantage of mass duplication, follow these steps:

1. **Select your object and enter interactive placement mode (Ctrl+B).**

2. **Press and hold your left mouse button to interactively move your selection around the map.**

3. **Press and release Shift.**

   Boom. You've just placed a duplicate object in your scene.

4. **Keep pressing and releasing Shift to add more duplicates under your cursor.**

   This is a very quick way to populate the environment on your map with objects like bushes.

Of course, the downside of cloning objects this way is that all the objects will have the same rotation, making your map look sterile and manufactured rather than natural and somewhat random. Fortunately, GIANTS Editor has a way to help, and it's also integrated with interactive placement mode.

To use it, select your object, enter interactive placement mode (Ctrl+B) and hold your left mouse button. Instead of pressing Shift to make a duplicate, press Ctrl. Doing this also places a duplicate object in your map as before, but now GIANTS Editor introduces some random rotation along your object's *y*-axis (usually the vertical axis). This method is a great way to populate your scene and give it a more varied, natural appearance. The following shows a quick rundown of the various options you have while in interactive placement mode.

Shortcut	Description
Left-click+drag	Interactively place selected object
Left-click+drag+Shift	Interactively place a duplicate
Left-click+drag+Ctrl	Interactively place a randomly rotated duplicate

Any time you add to your scene or duplicate an object, the new object is added at the end of your selection's parent group in the Scenegraph. Fortunately, the Scenegraph panel automatically scrolls to your selection, so it's pretty hard to get lost.

Organizing your map

You also want to consider overall organization when editing your map. Maps can be large and contain multiple areas, each populated with many objects. If you're not careful, you can easily find yourself in an incredibly disorganized jumble of a map. Wherever possible, keep a clean hierarchical organization. To facilitate this, GIANTS Editor incorporates a very useful tool, the transform group.

A *transform group* basically is way to organize a variety of loosely related objects. Say your map includes a small town with a little park at its center. You can take all of the objects in that park — fountains, benches, tables, trees, bushes, and so on — and collect them in a transform group. This way, if you have a need to select all objects at once, you only have to select that transform group in the Scenegraph. The icon for a transform group in the Scenegraph is a little group of shapes, specifically a square, triangle, and circle.

The transform group also provides you with a quick way of navigating around your map. Assume you have a transform group for every major area in your map. You can select that transform group in the Scenegraph and then press F to focus the 3D Viewport on that selection. Doing so is usually much faster than trying to fly around in the 3D Viewport looking for the area of the map you want to edit.

Choose Create⇨TransformGroup from the menu to add a new transform group, named *transform,* at the bottom of the Scenegraph. You can change the name of the transform group by selecting it and then editing the Name field in the Attributes panel.

New transform groups are empty, so you need to fill them. To move an object into a transform group, use the following steps:

1. **Select the desired object.**

   You can do this in either the 3D Viewport or the Scenegraph, whichever is most convenient.

2. **Cut the object.**

   Press Ctrl+X or choose Edit⇨Cut from the menu, and the object will disappear from the map. Don't worry, though, you'll add it back soon.

3. **Select the destination transform group in the Scenegraph.**

You want your object to be a part of this transform group.

4. Paste your object.

Press Ctrl+V or choose Edit⇨Paste from the menu. Voilá! Your object is back on the map, now organized as part of your new transform group.

 You also can nest transform groups. Taking the earlier example of the part in the center of a small town, you can take the park transform group and include it in a transform group of the rest of the town the same way you add any other object to a transform group.

Importing external assets

You're not limited to just working with the objects that are already included on a map. You can import new objects, too. These objects can be from other maps and mods, or they can be something you've created from scratch using 3D software such as Blender, Maya, or 3ds Max. See Chapter 7 for more on making custom 3D models for your mods.

Assuming the asset you want to import is properly formatted in either I3D or FBX format, bringing new assets into your map is as simple as choosing File⇨Import from the menu and navigating to the file you want using the file browser. Chapter 8 includes more detail on importing and exporting.

Adjusting User Attributes

In addition to the general settings available in the Attributes panel such as name, rotation, and visibility, any object in a Farming Simulator map can also have a set of custom, user-definable attributes. As a modder, you can use these powerful attributes for additional functionality, such as customizing scripts and triggers within the game. You can find these settings in the User Attributes panel (Window⇨User Attributes).

Probably the most common set of user attributes relate to fields. If you a have a map open in GIANTS Editor, select a field transform group from the Scenegraph. (Typically, you can find them nested inside a more general transform group, simply named *fields*.) With a field transform group selected, open the User Attributes panel and have a look. You should see something like Figure 2-2.

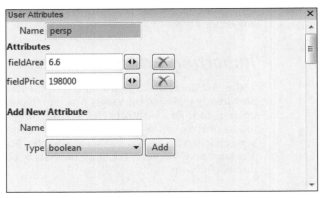

Figure 2-2: The User Attributes panel shows custom parameters for objects like fields.

Fields have two custom user attributes, *fieldArea* and *fieldPrice*. A trigger uses these attributes in-game to allow the player to purchase the field. By changing the *fieldPrice* user attribute on the field you currently have selected, for example, you can make it cheaper or more expensive for the player who uses your map. (Refer to the next section for more on triggers.)

Triggering Events in Your Map

Triggers are a big part of what makes a map interactive and fun to play in Farming Simulator. In short, a *trigger* is an object on your map that causes something to happen (an *event*) when the player activates it. A whole host of events can happen in the game: buying fields, filling trailers with water, loading silos, and so on. Even getting in-game help is an event. These events have triggers placed on the map or in the interface so the player can activate them.

Triggers usually have to be associated with one or more objects to be of any use. At the very least most triggers have an icon object that floats in the map so the player can see where it is and drive or walk to it. For example, a *fieldBuyTrigger* uses the user attributes of its parent's transform group along with some child objects to define the location, size, and price of a field. With those components, the trigger has all of the necessary information for when the player uses it to activate a field-buying event.

Because each trigger has slightly different requirements, the best way to include one on your map is to copy the full setup from another part of your map. The basic workflow looks something like this:

1. **Find the trigger you're interested in using.**

2. **Select its parent (usually an object or transform group).**

3. **Duplicate that object and place it on your map where you want.**

4. **Tweak and modify the trigger and user attributes as necessary.**

If you want to use a trigger that isn't already on your map, your easiest course of action is to find another map that uses that trigger. Then you can use this same process, but instead of duplicating in Step 3, you export the trigger from that map and import it into your map.

Chapter 3

Editing Surface Details in Maps

• •

In This Chapter

▶ Modifying the environment's look and feel

▶ Detailing the map with foliage and textures

▶ Mastering navigation meshes

• •

*T*he exciting part of map editing comes in the process of actually changing the landscape. Dig gullies. Build up hills or flatten them into fields. Create roads and small towns. Plant bushes and trees and make spaces for livestock to roam. Or give the player a real challenge by creating a desolate wasteland to farm.

A map is your world to create, and this chapter shows you the world-building tools available in GIANTS Editor.

Editing Terrain

The real fun comes in making real, actual changes to the topography of your map. Don't like that hill? Flatten it out! Want to introduce the challenge of terraced farming? Have at it! GIANTS Editor provides some very powerful terrain-editing tools that make all of this possible.

The Terrain Editing panel in GIANTS Editor controls the terrain-editing capabilities. The panel is hidden by default, so enable it by choosing Window⇨Terrain Editing from the menu. Figure 3-1 shows the various sections that are available to you in the Terrain Editing panel.

Figure 3-1: The Terrain Editing panel is divided into multiple sections.

As Figure 3-1 shows, the Terrain Editing panel is quite large. In fact, unless you're running GIANTS Editor on a large screen, seeing all of these panels at the same time won't be easy. You need to make good use of collapsing and expanding the sections within the panel. To toggle a section as expanded or collapsed, click the black arrow on the far right of the section's header bar. If the arrow is facing down, the section is expanded. If it's facing up, the section is collapsed.

Fortunately, the sections of the Terrain Editing panel are quite task oriented. You only need the first three panels (Brush, Noise, and Erosion) for surface sculpting, as described in the next section. For texture painting, you only need the Brush and Texture Layer Painting sections. The following sections take a closer look at how you can use the Terrain Editing panel.

Sculpting the surface

Now you can get your digital hands dirty and start shaping the surface of your map using the sculpting tools in GIANTS Editor. To begin sculpting, you must enter Terrain Sculpt Mode by clicking the icon in the toolbar that looks like a pair of hills with up and down arrows above them. It's the third button shown in Figure 3-2.

Figure 3-2: The mode toolbar with Terrain Sculpt Mode enabled.

After you enable Terrain Sculpt Mode, if you move your mouse cursor in the 3D Viewport, you should notice that a red circle that follows your cursor along the terrain's surface. This red circle is your terrain brush. Figure 3-3 shows the terrain brush in the 3D Viewport.

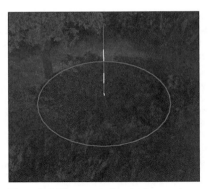

Figure 3-3: The terrain brush shows where you're sculpting in the 3D Viewport.

With the terrain brush, you can see exactly where you're sculpting on your map. The circle of the brush also defines the radius of influence that your brush has. You can increase and decrease the radius by using the scroll wheel on your mouse. Alternatively, you can also adjust the radius from the Brush section of the Terrain Editing panel.

At this point, you can jump right into sculpting with your mouse. The following list describes what each mouse button does by default:

✔ **Left mouse button (LMB):** Click and drag with the LMB to add to the surface of your terrain, effectively lifting it up.

✔ **Middle mouse button (MMB):** Clicking and dragging the MMB smooths the surface. You can usually access the MMB by pressing down on your mouse's scroll wheel.

✔ **Right mouse button (RMB):** The RMB subtracts from the terrain's surface, as if you were digging a hole or a trench in the ground.

Those are the default settings. From the Brush section of the Terrain Editing panel, you can access a variety of ways to customize the sculpt brush. Here's a quick rundown of the available settings:

- ✔ **Terrain:** Using this drop-down list, you can pick the specific terrain object you want to edit if your map has more than one.

- ✔ **Radius:** This setting controls the influence area of your brush.

- ✔ **Opacity:** When sculpting, the opacity is multiplied by the value setting.

- ✔ **Hardness:** With this setting, you can control your brush's *fall-off,* or how abruptly the brush's influence area affects your terrain. Low values are gentler and merge more smoothly. High values give sharper edges.

- ✔ **Value:** Think of value as your brush's strength. Crank it up and you can have a mountain in seconds. Keep it low and you can make subtler, detailed changes.

- ✔ **Brush Type:** You have two choices here:

    - • **Round brush:** The round brush works best for organic areas.

    - • **Square brush:** The square brush is more suitable for adjusting terrain around man-made objects, like buildings.

Using the Replace brush

The Brush section also gives you the ability to change the key mappings for your left, right, and middle mouse buttons. You can actually change any mouse button to have one of five different brush behaviors: Add, Smooth, Subtract, Replace, and Remove. (I discuss Add, Smooth, and Subtract in the previous section as the default values for each mouse button, whereas Remove is more relevant to painting foliage, which I discuss in the "Painting

Foliage and Ground Details" section later in this chapter.) However, the Replace behavior is very interesting for terrain sculpting.

You can change any mouse button's behavior from the Brush section. Click the drop-down menu next to LMB, MMB, or RMB to bind a different brush behavior to any of those mouse buttons.

If you change the left mouse button to use the Replace behavior, GIANTS Editor will push or pull all terrain under your brush to a specific height, as defined by the Replace value in the Brush section of the Terrain Editing panel. This brush is incredibly useful if you need to flatten out part of your terrain. Think about using it not only for terraces and plateaus, but also for in-town areas, such as roads or parking lots.

You can also quickly set the Replace value by moving the brush over the terrain in the 3D Viewport and pressing Ctrl+R. Doing so sets the Replace value to match the height at that part of the terrain.

You can further customize the Replace behavior using the Replace Limit drop-down list in the Terrain Editing panel's Brush section. You have three choices:

- ✔ **None:** The default value. All terrain, whether higher or lower than the Replace value, is raised or dropped to match accordingly.

- ✔ **Lower:** Only parts of the terrain that are *lower* than the Replace value are adjusted and lifted. Any part of the surface that's above that value remains untouched.

- ✔ **Higher:** Only parts of the terrain that are *higher* than the Replace value are adjusted and brought down. Any part of the terrain that's below that value remains untouched.

Generating seed values

Computers can't generate truly random values. To get around this, programmers and computer scientists developed psuedorandom algorithms for generating a value that appears to be random. It's not quite real randomness because there's a prescribed and repeatable means of arriving at that value, but it's random enough to be useful in most general cases (such as adding noise to a terrain map).

A key component of most pseudorandom algorithms is a *seed value,* which is a base number that generates psuedorandom values. What's even crazier is that even the seed value can be psuedorandomly generated (the seed for that is typically something that's constantly changing, like your computer's system clock). Anyhow, this background information is at least somewhat useful when making adjustments to noise while sculpting.

Incorporating randomness with noise

At the opposite side of the spectrum from the Replace brush behavior is the ability to add noise. You occasionally may want to put in some random surface variation while sculpting. You want the terrain to appear more natural and rugged. If so, activate the Enable Noise checkbox in the Terrain Editing panel.

With noise enabled, you can start adding natural surface variations to your terrain sculpt. However, when you start, you may not notice much difference because the default noise values are pretty small. The following list describes each value in the Noise section of the Terrain Editing panel:

✔ **Seed:** By default, this value is set to zero, but it can be any integer value. You may want to change the seed value periodically while you sculpt by clicking the Random Seed button. Doing so can help prevent having any kind of visible pattern in your noise, thereby ensuring a more natural-looking rough surface.

✔ **Persistence:** Think of persistence as the strength value of your noise. The higher the persistence, the more influence the noise has over your Add or Subtract brush behavior. If you turn the persistence value all the way up to 1, your brush will appear to both add and subtract, regardless of the behavior you've chosen.

✔ **Frequency:** This parameter controls just how much noise occurs within your brush's influence area. High frequency values add more up and down variations within that area, whereas low frequency values have less variation. You may not be able to take full advantage of high frequency values unless you use a very large brush because the geometry of your terrain may not be fine enough to take advantage of that additional variation.

✔ **Octaves:** Consider the numbers in this drop-down list as multiplication factors for your noise. The more octaves, the more dramatic the noise influence. If you want subtle variation, use a lower octave value.

The noise feature only works on the Add and Subtract brush behaviors. It doesn't have any influence on the Smooth or Replace behaviors.

Adding surface erosion

Direct, traditional sculpting is a fantastic, tried-and-true way of customizing map terrains, especially if you want to make man-made terrain adjustments. In the natural world, terrain does change over time using some fairly simple rules regarding erosion. Ironically, reproducing these effects with traditional sculpting methods can be quite tedious. For that reason, GIANTS Editor includes Erosion parameters for editing terrain.

Erosion settings only work on the Add brush behavior.

Generally speaking, erosion makes steep slopes even steeper while flattening terrain at the bottom of the slope. After you enable the erosion settings by toggling the Enable Erosion checkbox in the Terrain Editing panel, GIANTS Editor offers two forms of erosion:

✔ **Thermal:** Thermal erosion simulates how dirt and rock break loose over time and slide down a slope to form a pile at the bottom. For this reason thermal erosion only works with the Add brush behavior on terrain that has a slope greater than 45°.

✔ **Hydraulic:** This type of erosion tends to be the most useful. Using hydraulic erosion and the Add brush behavior, you can quickly sculpt a creek bed or road-side ditch. Crank up the values in the Erosion section of the Terrain Editing panel and you can find yourself sculpting a system of canyons.

If you try to add erosion over a cultivated section of terrain (where crops are growing, or ready to be grown), it may appear as if nothing is happening. Don't be fooled. If you move the 3D Viewport camera below the surface of your terrain, you can notice that your erosion sculpting has definitely affected the terrain's surface. Those surface variations are reflected in the textures and geometry of that cultivated area.

Painting textures

If you started with an existing map, you may now have a road texture that runs over a mountain range, rock textures where you want a grassy field, or raw dirt that should be a park. You can fix everything by using the texture painting tools in GIANTS Editor.

To start painting textures, enable Terrain Detail Texture Paint Mode from the toolbar, which is the button with an icon that looks like a red pencil writing on a couple of hills. Look at Figure 3-2 and the Terrain Detail Texture Paint Mode button is the fourth button in the Mode toolbar.

Because you're painting textures now, I suggest that you collapse the Noise and Erosion sections of the Terrain Editing panel. You only need the sections for Brush and Texture Layer Painting.

When you enable Terrain Detail Texture Paint Mode, take notice of two important changes in the 3D Viewport:

✓ **Your brush now rotates to match the angle of your terrain surface.** When sculpting, the brush always points straight down. When painting, however, the brush matches the surface normal beneath its area of influence, which means that although you can't sculpt sideways, you can certainly paint that way.

✓ **A grid of white lines is overlaid on the terrain.** This grid defines *terrain chunks* on your map. Within the boundaries of each chunk, you can only use a maximum of four different textures. To help you, included with the grid are text overlays that tell you which textures (and their corresponding coverage percentages) are used in a particular chunk.

In general, painting textures isn't all that different from sculpting your terrain, with just a few notable differences:

✓ The Opacity setting in the Brush section of the Terrain Editing panel (refer to Figure 3-1, earlier in this chapter) is a lot more useful. It controls how transparent each stroke of texture paint is on your map. Using this setting, you can mix textures to create a more naturally varied surface (and somewhat hide the fact that you only have four textures available per chunk).

✓ Another notable difference is in the Replace brush behavior. Unless Opacity is set to zero, the Replace behavior completely disregards it. So instead of mixing your painted texture with what's already there, this brush behavior simply replaces it. The Replace height value and Replace Limit drop-down menu have no effect in Terrain Detail Texture Paint Mode.

In the Texture Layer Painting section of the Terrain Editing panel, you have a few additional controls that can aid in your texture painting process. The following list describes each of them:

- **Slope Limit Start/End:** These values, measured in degrees, give you control over where your textures appear, relative to the slope of your terrain's surface. For example, say you sculpt an area that you mean to be grassy with a few rocky outcroppings. Assume that you already painted the whole area with a grass texture and you want your rock texture to appear anywhere it's not flat (those spots should stay grassy). To do that, bump up the Slope Limit Start setting to something greater than zero and then start painting. This method is a fast way to paint terrain realistically.

- **Chunk Vis:** This checkbox toggles the visibility of the terrain chunk grid.

- **Chunk Vis Dist:** The chunk visibility distance controls how far away you can see the chunk grid in your map. Sometimes you need to see the grid for up-close areas, but the grid in the distance is just distracting. This parameter helps get around that issue.

- **Texture Layer:** You use the Texture Layer drop-down menu setting the most in this section. This menu lets you choose any of the available textures in your map to paint. Just be aware of the four-texture limit per terrain chunk and pay attention to the textures that are already in use on a particular chunk.

If you want to take a texture out of a chunk, select the Remove brush behavior and click anywhere in the chunk. When you click, the your active texture is removed from that chunk and you're then free to add a new texture.

Painting Foliage and Ground Details

You're in Farming Simulator after all, so you probably are interested in setting up some fields and crops. Adding foliage and ground details follows the same basic process as sculpting and texture painting, though it also has its own little bag of tricks.

Unlike texture painting, you don't need to concern yourself with terrain chunks and limiting what you paint per chunk. However, foliage types and growth states are entirely controlled by toggling channels on a *bitmask,* or a series of 1s and 0s with an encoded meaning. Don't worry, though, it's not as complex as it sounds.

To start painting foliage or ground details, enable Terrain Foliage Paint Mode in GIANTS Editor by clicking the button with a plant icon in the toolbar. Referring to Figure 3-2, the Terrain Foliage Paint Mode button is the last button in the Mode toolbar.

After you activate the Terrain Foliage Paint Mode, you should notice that, like Terrain Sculpt Mode, you have a brush in the 3D Viewport under the mouse cursor that always points down. In the Terrain Editing panel, you only need to concern yourself with the Brush and Foliage Layer Painting sections, so you can collapse the other sections of the Terrain Editing panel.

Because you're creating a map on which other people can play Farming Simulator, make sure you consider the state of the terrain as a starting point for the player. Do you want players to have to build everything from the beginning or do you want to provide them with mostly grown crops to keep things easy? Because you're a modder now, you have to turn off the gamer part of your brain a little bit. Sure, modding in shortcuts is interesting for a little while, but your real focus is on making a map that's fun to play. This includes incorporating a bit of challenge so the player doesn't get bored.

After changing the foliage on an existing map, you need to start a new game in Farming Simulator with that map. If you don't and choose to play an older saved game with this map, then the changes to foliage won't show up when you play.

Creating farmable land

Approach the process of creating fields the same way you would if you were farming in real life. Just use this simple two-step procedure:

1. Prepare the land for planting.

2. Plant your crops.

This section covers the first of these two steps. With Terrain Foliage Paint Mode enabled, go to the Foliage Layer Painting section of the Terrain Editing panel and choose terrainDetail from the Foliage Layer drop-down menu.

Here's where things get a bit tricky. Look at the Foliage Layer Painting section of the Terrain Editing panel and notice an array of checkboxes, each with a number next to it. These checkboxes are your *foliage channels,* the bitmask that defines what your foliage brush paints on the map.

For the terrainDetail foliage layer, you only use channels 0 through 6. Channels 0, 1, 2, and 3 define the type of terrain detail you're painting. These are *exclusive channels*, meaning that you should enable only one of them at a time. That is, if channel 1 is enabled, make sure 0, 2, and 3 are disabled. Table 3-1 shows the type of ground detail each of these first four channels enables.

Table 3-1	Foliage Channels for the terrainDetail Layer
Channel	*Ground Detail*
0	Cultivated land
1	Ploughed land
2	Seeded/planted land
3	Seeded/planted potatoes

Channels 4 through 6 aren't exclusive; you can mix them with each other as well as any of the other channels. Table 3-2 explains these channel controls, as well as channel combinations.

Table 3-2	Control Channels for the terrainDetail Foliage Layer
Channel	*Ground Detail*
4	Sprayed/fertilized land
5	Rotate detail texture 45° clockwise
6	Rotate detail texture 90°
5+6	Rotate detail texture 45° counterclockwise

For example, if you want to have seeded terrain that's been fertilized and rotated by 45° clockwise, you would enable the checkboxes for channels 2, 4, and 5.

To actually paint the ground detail in your map, find a relatively even area and left-click + drag your mouse cursor as if you were texture painting. You can change the terrain back to its precultivated level using your right mouse button, essentially erasing your foliage and terrain detail back to its raw state. You can also use this erase operation by disabling all of your foliage channels, but doing so is a much slower process.

Adding plant life

To include foliage to your land, use the exact same steps for painting foliage as you would for painting terrain detail. From the Foliage Layer Painting section of the Terrain Editing panel:

1. **Choose your foliage layer.**

2. **Adjust the foliage channel bitmask to control details.**

3. **Paint your foliage.**

The foliage channels are more complex for plant life than they are for ground details. For plant life, the first four channels (0 through 3) control the type of plant. The next row of channels (4 through 7) dictates that plant's growth state. In the third row of channels, only channel 8 has any effect. It defines whether the crop is in a windrow (a row of cut vegetation, ready to be baled or stored) or not. Table 3-3 covers the various states of the first row of foliage channels.

Table 3-3   Foliage Channel Settings for Various Farming Simulator Crops

Foliage Channels	Type of Crop
0	Wheat
1	Grass
2	Barley
3	Sugar beet
0+1	Rape (canola)
0+2	Maize (corn)
1+2	Dry grass
1+2+3	Potato

Fortunately, GIANTS Editor helps you out a bit here. When choosing the crop you want from the Foliage Layer drop-down menu, it automatically sets the bitmask for the first four foliage channels. Growth states for each type of plant is a different matter. Table 3-4 attempts to show all of the various growth state values for each type of crop.

Table 3-4	Matrix of Growth States for Each Type of Crop			
Bits	**Normal Crops**	**Grass**	**Potato**	**Sugar beet**
4	State A	State A	State A	State A
5	State B	State B	State B	State B
4+5	State C	State C	State C	State C
6	State D	State D	State D	State D
4+6	Fully grown	Fully grown	Growing (sowing width)	Fully grown
5+6	Fully grown	Fully grown	Fully grown (sowing width)	Fully grown
4+5+6	Fully grown	Fully grown	N/A	Fully grown
7	Withered	Fully grown	N/A	Withered
4+7	Cut short	Fully grown	Cut short (sowing)	N/A
5+7	N/A	Fully grown	Prepared for cutting (sowing width)	Prepared for cutting

Painting ground details and foliage can be a time-consuming process. Don't forget to save your work on your map as you go.

Working with Navigation Meshes: Adding Spaces for Animals

Plants aren't the only things that can be grown on a farm. You can also designate areas of your map for raising various types of livestock. The default map offers the capabilities for cows, sheep, and chickens. Of course, other mods out there allow players to raise other types of animals as well. I'm still hoping to build a velociraptor farm. (Hey, a guy can dream, right?)

In any case, just like you need to prepare terrain in your maps for growing crops, you have to go through a similar process for raising livestock on your map. You do this with navigation meshes. A *navigation mesh* is special geometry on a map that defines where a specific type of animal is allowed to roam.

Navigation meshes are hidden from view when you first launch GIANTS Editor. In order to make them visible in your map, choose View⇨Show⇨Navigation Meshes from the menu. Figure 3-4 shows the navigation mesh for some chickens.

You may notice at this point that you can't select a navigation mesh in the 3D Viewport. So centering the view on that navigation mesh can be a bit difficult. The easy workaround, however, is to select a building or object near the navigation mesh and focus the view on that by pressing F. From there, you can orbit, pan, and zoom the camera to get a better view.

Figure 3-4: Navigation meshes, when made visible, appear in your map as large blue areas.

The following sections explain how you can create and modify navigation meshes so animals can happily roam on your map's farm and avoid walking through buildings and other obstacles.

Painting information

Not only are you unable to select navigation meshes in the 3D Viewport, you also can't directly manipulate and edit navigation meshes. Instead, you must generate navigation meshes by painting on the terrain.

Rather than painting textures or foliage, you're painting information. In the Terrain Editing panel, your main focus should be on the Info Layer Painting section. To begin painting your navigation mesh, enable Terrain Info Layer Paint Mode from the toolbar, which is the button that looks like a blue pencil drawing on some hills. Refer to Figure 3-2, where the Terrain Info Layer Painting Mode button is the second to last among the Mode tools.

As with the foliage painting and sculpting modes, activating Terrain Info Layer Painting Mode gets you a downward-facing brush under your mouse cursor in the 3D Viewport. Painting on the info layer is very similar to foliage painting in that you're painting based on a bitmask of a set of channels. These channels are all controlled from the Info Layer Painting section of the Terrain Editing panel. The info layer channels aren't complex. In fact, for the default map, you use only the first three info channels (0 through 2). Table 3-5 shows the channel mapping for the default navigation mesh types.

Table 3-5	Info Channels for Painting Navigation Meshes
Channel	*Type of Livestock*
0	Cows
1	Sheep
2	Chickens

These channels are exclusive. If channel 1 is enabled, then channels 0 and 2 should be disabled.

Assuming that you're editing an existing navigation mesh, after you choose the correct info channel that you want to paint, you should notice the area around that navigation mesh becomes gray. This area is the *info paint* that was used to generate the original navigation mesh. Using the familiar painting mouse buttons (LMB to add, RMB to subtract), you can paint a new shape for your navigation mesh.

The info layer paint is always done in blocky squares, so you can't get too organic with the shape of your navigation mesh. When GIANTS Editor generates the mesh, it smooths some of those jagged edges for you.

Defining navigation mesh boundaries for objects

As you paint the info layer for your navigation mesh, you may find it tedious to paint around buildings and small props. In fact, GIANTS Editor can help you automatically avoid those objects. You can tell the object to build a *navigation mesh mask* for you. Then, when you re-create the navigation mesh, the editor takes account of the mask for each object.

To define the navigation mesh mask for an object, hop out of Terrain Info Layer Paint Mode (just click the button for it again in the toolbar). Now select the object you want the navigation mesh to avoid and look in the Attributes panel. Specifically, you want to look at the Shape tab in the Attributes panel, as shown in Figure 3-5.

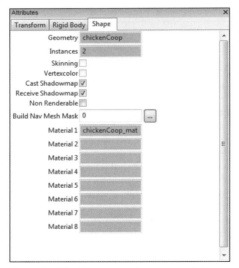

Figure 3-5: The Shape tab allows you to define a navigation mesh mask for an object.

To set the navigation mesh mask for your object, click the button with the ellipsis (. . .) to the right of the Build Nav Mesh Mask field. Doing so pops up a dialog like the one in Figure 3-6.

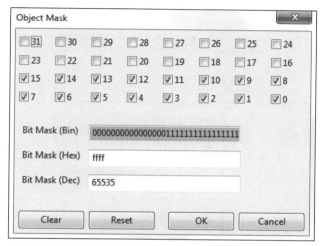

Figure 3-6: The Shape Build Nav Mesh Mask dialog.

From the dialog window, select the info channel that corresponds to the animal your navigation mesh is controlling. In Figure 3-6, channel 2 is enabled, meaning chickens. When you're done, click OK.

Generating your navigation mesh

To re-create or rebuild your navigation mesh, you need to select it. Although you can't select the navigation mesh in the 3D Viewport, you can still select the navigation mesh from the Scenegraph. Of course, on a large map with many objects, doing so can certainly be a challenge. On a well-organized map, however, doing so is a bit easier.

For example, on maps that come with Farming Simulator, there's a transform group named *animals* and within that transform group are transform groups for raising each type of livestock on the map. Those groups are typically named something like *cowsHusbandry* or *chickenHusbandry*. Within those transform groups, you can find any navigation meshes for that animal type. As Figure 3-7 shows, the icon for a navigation mesh looks like four squares in a grid, connected with lines.

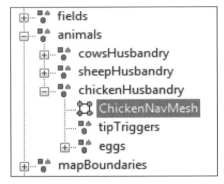

Figure 3-7: You can select navigation meshes from the Scenegraph.

After selecting your navigation mesh, you need to rebuild it. To do so, choose Create⇨Navigation Mesh from the menu. You'll then get a dialog like the one shown in Figure 3-8.

For the most part, you can keep the values in this dialog at their defaults. The three that you're most interested in are the following:

✔ **Radius field (under Agent):** The Radius value defines a perimeter around your navigation mesh based on the size of the animal. Using the correct value prevents animals from walking through objects in your map. Table 3-6 gives radius values for the three animals available in maps that ship with Farming Simulator.

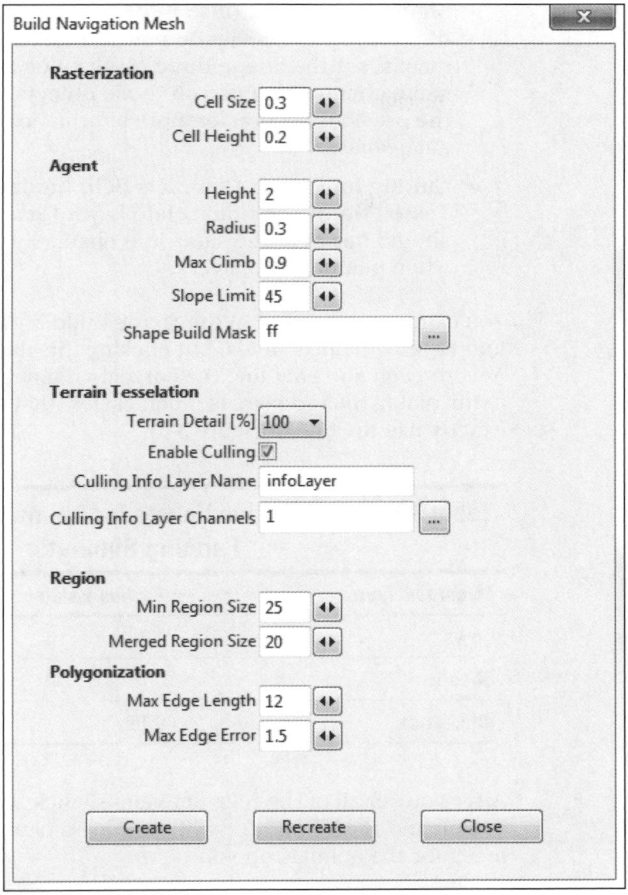

Build Navigation Mesh ✕

Rasterization

Cell Size `0.3` ◄►

Cell Height `0.2` ◄►

Agent

Height `2` ◄►

Radius `0.3` ◄►

Max Climb `0.9` ◄►

Slope Limit `45` ◄►

Shape Build Mask `ff` `...`

Terrain Tesselation

Terrain Detail [%] `100` ▼

Enable Culling ☑

Culling Info Layer Name `infoLayer`

Culling Info Layer Channels `1` `...`

Region

Min Region Size `25` ◄►

Merged Region Size `20` ◄►

Polygonization

Max Edge Length `12` ◄►

Max Edge Error `1.5` ◄►

[Create]   [Recreate]   [Close]

Figure 3-8: The Build Navigation Mesh dialog is where you can rebuild existing navigation meshes or create new ones.

✔ **Shape Build Mask (also under Agent):** If you have objects in your navigation mesh that build shape masks, set the Shape Build Mask value to use the same channel you use on those objects. Refer to the previous section for more information on building shape masks.

✔ **Culling Info Layer Channels field (under Terrain Tesselation):** The Culling Info Layer Channels value should be set to the same info channel you used when painting info layers.

You can type a number in the Shape Build Mask or Culling Info Layer Channels fields, but clicking the ellipsis button next to each and enabling the correct channel checkbox in the dialog that appears is much easier (that dialog looks exactly like the one in Figure 3-6).

Table 3-6	Radius Values for Animals in Farming Simulator
Livestock Type	*Radius Value*
Cows	1.2
Sheep	0.7
Chickens	0.15

After you set all of the relevant values, click the Recreate button and GIANTS Editor will generate a new navigation mesh for the animals on your map.

Keep the area of your navigation mesh reasonable. Generating the navigation mesh can be a memory-intensive process for the computer and on large navigation meshes, your computer may not have enough RAM.

Chapter 4

Using the Material Panel

In This Chapter

▶ Tweaking materials on your mod

▶ Visualizing texture maps from within GIANTS Editor

*T*he process of adding textures and defining materials on 3D objects can be pretty involved. In fact, Chapter 9 focuses on creating and adding textures. A *texture* is simply an image. The image's colors control how light from within the game engine interacts with the surface of a 3D model. The collection of textures and attributes that defines — refers to "collection" this interaction is called a *material*. A 3D model can have multiple materials. In GIANTS Engine, a 3D object can have up to eight materials defined by that object's geometry.

Whether you're building textures and materials from scratch or simply tweaking the settings on an existing model, you do the final adjustments to your material from within GIANTS Editor. After all, GIANTS Editor is the best place to preview what the object is going to look like in-game without actually loading the game.

Modifying Material Properties

In GIANTS Editor, the Material panel is where you can make the necessary tweaks you want; however, the Material panel isn't visible when you launch GIANTS Editor. To enable it, go to the Window menu (Window⇨Material Editing). After enabling it, the Material panel's default position is docked at the bottom of the Scenegraph.

This layout can be a bit cramped, so you may find it more useful to drag the Material panel and dock it to another part of the interface or leave it in its own floating window. Wherever you decide to put the Material panel, GIANTS Editor can remember where you leave it for the next time you open it. Figure 4-1 shows the Material panel.

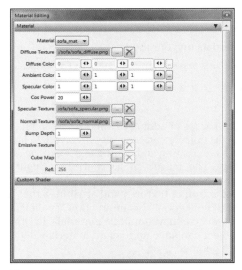

Figure 4-1: The Material Editing panel is where you can modify a model's textures and material settings.

Generally speaking, a 3D object's materials are defined in a 3D-modeling program outside of GIANTS Editor, such as Blender or Maya. The Material panel gives you the ability to adjust and troubleshoot these materials so they look their absolute best when they're loaded in Farming Simulator.

When it comes to GIANTS Engine, you need to consider
three primary material settings:

- ✔ **Diffuse Color:** This is the base color of your material.
  Think about it as the color that the material most
  wants to be, and the color that's most apparent under
  normal lighting conditions. In other words, the *diffuse
  color* is a single flat color over the entire material or
  varied colors defined by a texture map.

- ✔ **Ambient Color:** The best way to think of *ambient
  color* is to consider it the hue that influences the
  material's diffuse color when no additional light is in
  the scene. Typically you want your ambient color to
  be set to white (1, 1, 1 in the Material panel's interface). The ambient color can only be a single flat
  color; it can't be defined by a texture.

- ✔ **Specular Color:** A material's specular properties
  pertain to its highlights when a light shines upon it.
  The *specular color* is the color of those highlights.
  Like ambient color, specular color can only be a
  single flat hue; however, you can use a grayscale
  image texture to control the amount of specularity.
  That is, you can control how shiny different parts
  of a 3D model appear using a specular texture map.
  (See Chapter 9 for a few more clever tricks you can
  pull with the specular map.) You can also modify the
  overall shininess of your material by adjusting the
  Cos Power slider.

You can adjust any of these colors from the Material
panel. The three numeric text fields next to each color
label in the Material panel represent the influence of each
of the red, green, and blue (RGB) primaries, on a scale
from 0 to 1. So as an example, putting a 0 in each field of
the diffuse color sets that color to black. Putting each of
them to 0.5 results in a middle gray.

Now, you *can* twiddle these values to get the color you want, but clicking the button with the ellipsis (. . .) next to the right of these text fields is much easier. Doing so opens a color picker window, as Figure 4-2 shows.

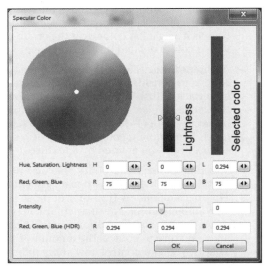

Figure 4-2: The color picker allows you to select a specular color for your material.

Although the color picker also has a bunch of number fields that you can mess with, the easiest way to select a color is to click and drag your cursor within the circular color wheel until you land on the color you want. Your current selected color appears in a strip on the far right of the color picker window. You can adjust the color's darkness or lightness by clicking and dragging within the Lightness slider to the right of the color wheel.

Comprehending colors in computer graphics

In nearly all computer game environments, colors are defined using the three primary colors of light: red, green, and blue (RGB) rather than the three pigment primaries you may have studied in grade school (red, yellow, and blue).

Basically, computer monitors produce color by emitting light. As such, working with the primary colors of light makes the most sense to get an accurate representation of what you see on the screen.

Viewing Material Textures

The Material panel also gives you the ability to view and change textures on 3D objects in your mod. This is particularly useful if you've converted the PNG texture images exported from your 3D modeling software to the recommended DirectDraw Surface (DDS) format (see Chapter 9 for more on using DDS) and you need to point your mod to those new textures.

GIANTS Engine supports three main texture types:

✔ **Diffuse Texture Map:** This is an image texture that defines variable diffuse colors over the surface of a 3D object. If you want to have more than one solid color over the surface of your 3D object, you want to use a diffuse texture rather than the simple flat diffuse color.

✔ **Specular Texture Map:** In its simplest form, the specular texture image isn't full color. Instead, this grayscale image defines the material's shininess. Lighter pixels define a shinier area whereas darker pixels stipulate a more matte surface. The latest version of GIANTS Engine supports a more complex type of specular texture. See Chapter 9 for details.

↙ **Normal Texture Map:** You may wonder if the other textures are abnormal textures. That's not quite the case. In fact, the normal texture is the strangest of the three major texture types. In 3D graphics, a *normal* is an imaginary line that projects perpendicular to the surface of a triangle. These normals are used to calculate how light reacts with the surface of the 3D object. If you can modify them, you can make some pretty dramatic changes to how light interacts with your material, which is exactly what normal maps do. Normal maps allow you to show the illusion of more surface detail (such as bumps and ridges) than is present in the object's actual geometry.

If you click on the ellipsis (. . .) button to the right of the text field, GIANTS Editor shows you a preview of the current texture and gives you the ability to search for a different texture image using a file browser interface. Figure 4-3 shows the Texture Viewer window.

Figure 4-3: The Texture Viewer showing a diffuse texture map.

Chapter 5

Playing with Particles

. . . .

In This Chapter

▶ Knowing the best place to use particles

▶ Editing particles

. . . .

*A*n integrated particle editor is my favorite part in a computer graphics program. *Particles* are just simply fun. They're dynamically generated so you don't have to worry about animating them by hand. They incorporate at least a little bit of physics, so they can add realism to most scenes. And they're really easy to edit in real time by just pushing some sliders around. In fact, I've been known to spend hours just making particle systems do funny things that make me giggle. This chapter shares some of the fun that particles can be for you when building your mods.

Discovering the Uses for Particles

Particles provide a sense of realism and help the player feel immersed in the game. Because particle systems are dynamically generated, they can introduce a bit of random behavior to a map or a mod, making things feel more natural and real.

In a practical sense, particles are great any time you have a bunch of smaller things projecting from a single point, such as smoke from a fire, exhaust from a vehicle, seed from a harvester, or water from a fountain.

Specific to Farming Simulator, you can use particles in these two scenarios:

✔ **Adding life to an otherwise static scene.** Need a smoking fire pit at a campsite? A waterfall? A decorative fountain sculpture in a town square? These examples are excellent opportunities to use particles that run constantly.

✔ **Showing that something is being done.** Want to show that a vehicle is running by spewing a bit of exhaust? Show that a sprayer is actively fertilizing a field? Or perhaps let the player know potatoes are being harvested? These particle systems can be turned off and on at will, depending on what's happening in the game.

Other interesting possibilities are available for particles. I hope these ideas can get you thinking about some of the things you can add in your own mods.

Working with the Particle Editor

Opening up an existing particle system and playing with its settings is the best way to understand how particles work in GIANTS Editor. One of my favorites to play with is the waterfall particle system that ships with Farming Simulator 2015.

You can find it with the maps wherever you have Farming Simulator installed on your hard drive (on a Windows computer, it should be something like `C:\Program Files\ Farming Simulator 2015\data\maps\particle Systems\waterfallParticleSystem.i3d`). If you open that I3D file in GIANTS Editor and click the Play button in the toolbar, you can see the particle system start to work. Figure 5-1 shows a screenshot of what you should see in your 3D Viewport.

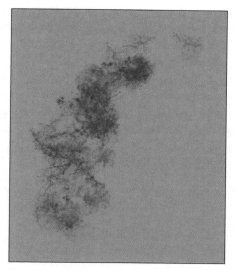

Figure 5-1: The waterfall particle simulation playing in the GIANTS Editor 3D Viewport.

To better see the particle system in action, you may want to temporarily add a light to the scene using Create⇨Light from the menu. (It's a temporary light because you don't want to save this I3D file with the light in it. Otherwise that light will show up in the game, making everything look brighter than you want.)

To play with the particle system, follow these steps:

1. **Enable the Particle System panel by going to Window⇨Particle System in the GIANTS Editor menu.**

    Doing so gets you a large panel with all sorts of parameters available for adjusting. Depending on how much screen real estate you have, you may need to collapse the various sections within the panel.

The values in the Particle System panel don't make much sense until you actually select a particle system.

2. Look in the Scenegraph.

Find the object named waterfallParticleSystem_emitter1.

3. Select that object and note that the selection in the 3D Viewport looks a bit weird.

It has all kinds of crazy squares around the splotchy water bits, like Figure 5-2 shows.

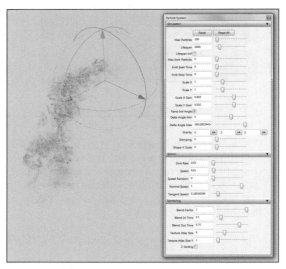

Figure 5-2: A selected particle system and the Particle System panel.

You can adjust different parameters to get your particle system working like you want (refer to Figure 5-2). The following list is a quick explanation of each section and the most useful parameters within each one:

The lowdown on those squares

To understand the funny-looking squares in your selected particle system, you need to know a bit about how particle systems work. The simple version is that there's an emitter object floating somewhere in 3D space. That _emitter_ spits out copies of little 3D points, called _particles._

Each particle has its own personal location, rotation, and scale defined by the overall particle system's parameters. Those particles act as parents for other 3D objects. In the case of this waterfall system, each particle owns a _billboard,_ or a textured 3D plane that always has its flat side facing the camera. Those billboards are the squares you see when the particle system is selected from the Scenegraph.

✔ **Simulation:** These are your main controls. They cover the overall nature of your particle system's behavior.

- **Reset/Reset All:** Changes to particle systems are sometimes hard to see in real time. These buttons return the particle system to a home state to have a clean start.

- **Max Particles:** As the name implies, Max Particles is the total number of particles from this system that show up at once. As an example, if your particle system is simulating grain, this should be high. If it's potatoes, it should be low.

- **Lifespan:** This is the amount of time, in milliseconds, that a single particle is on-screen, or _alive._ After that time goes by, the particle disappears.

- **Max Emit Particles:** The total number of particles that this particle system can emit when it's triggered. For example, you may have a mod with a dispenser that only provides something in fixed increments, such as a potato cannon. If you happen to make a potato cannon for your mod, it would only launch one potato at a time, so Max Emit Particles would be 1. With this parameter set, the particle system runs until it hits this number and then stops until triggered again.

- **Emit Start/Stop Time:** You can control when a particle system stops and starts, relative to being triggered.

- **Scale X/Y:** Treat these parameters as the starting size for the billboards.

- **Scale X/Y Gain:** These values control how much a particle grows each millisecond of its life. If your particle system is for things that don't change size (like food), these parameters should be set to zero.

- **Delta Angle Min/Max:** If you enable the random initialization angle (Rand Init Angle) checkbox, these two parameters define how much a billboard may be rotated from its initial state when it's born.

- **Gravity:** The three text fields next to this label correspond to forces in the X, Y, and Z directions. Because GIANTS Editor (and Farming Simulator) treats the *y*-axis as up and down, if you want realistic gravity, the *y*-axis value should be negative.

- **Damping:** *Damping* is a value that represents the amount of resistance (often because of friction) in physics. If your particle system is moving as you like, but just a bit out of control, you can increase the damping value and tone down a bit.

✔ **Spawn:** Whereas the Simulation section covers the overall particle simulation, the Spawn section has more direct controls over how each particle is born.

- **Emit Rate:** With this parameter, you control how frequently new particles are born from the emitter.

- **Speed:** You can control the velocity of particles as they come out of the emitter. Low values drip out, high values produce a fire hose.

- **Speed Random:** It's sometimes more natural looking if everything isn't moving at the same speed. Increasing this value introduces some variation to the speed of new particles.

- **Normal/Tangent Speed:** These two parameters dictate the initial direction that a particle goes when spawned.

🖝 **Rendering:** Quite possibly the most important section, the Rendering section controls how the player sees particles.

- **Blend Factor:** This parameter controls how transparent the billboards appear, regardless of the texture on them. Lower numbers are more transparent, higher numbers are more opaque.

- **Blend In/Out Time:** You can vary the transparency of a particle over the course of its life. For instance, smoke dissipates over time. So having smoke particles gradually fading out over their lifespans makes sense.

Adding Particles in Your Mod

The absolute easiest way to get a particle system added to your mod is to copy in an existing particle system into your mod. You can do this all from within GIANTS Editor using the following steps:

1. Open an existing particle system in GIANTS Editor.

You can choose one from another mod or from the maps that ship with Farming Simulator. For example, you can open `C:\Program Files\Farming Simulator 2015\data\maps\particleSystems\ smokeParticleSystem.i3D` to open a simple smoke particle system.

2. **From the Scenegraph, select the particle system that you want to use.**

3. **Choose File⇨Export Selection with Files from the menu.**

   Using the File Browser dialog, navigate to your mod's folder on your hard drive and then click the Save button.

4. **Open your mod in GIANTS Editor.**

   If prompted to save the particle system file, *do not save it.* Doing so may make Farming Simulator or the mod you're pulling the particle system from unplayable.

5. **Choose File⇨Import from the menu and use the dialog to navigate to the particle system file you just exported.**

You can also use the drag-and-drop features of your operating system to import the I3D file into your mod. Simply find the file in the system file browser (Windows Explorer in Windows, or Finder in Mac OS X) and drag the file into GIANTS Editor. Doing so automatically imports the particle system into your current scene. After you have the particle system in your mod's I3D file, you can start tweaking it and adjusting it to suit your mod's needs as the previous section describes.

One thing that you definitely want to change is the material on the particle system's emitter object. You need to open the Material panel and change the path to the Diffuse Texture Map (refer to Chapter 4).

If you're having trouble making the billboards in your particle system fully opaque (say, for a conveyor belt loaded with fruits), it may be because you imported a particle system designed for smoke or water. These particle systems vary the transparency of the billboard texture over time. The settings aren't in the Material panel, but instead they're in the Particle System panel, under Rendering. If you adjust the Blend Factor to 1.0, for example, your particles will be fully opaque for their full lifetime.

Part II

Creating Custom 3D Mods

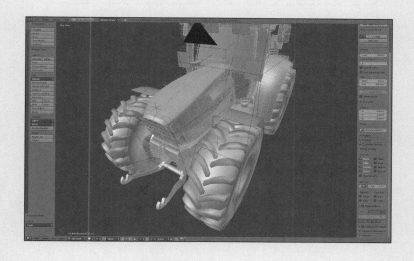

In this part . . .

✔ Understand what a `modDesc.xml` file is, why it's necessary for a mod, and how to set up on of your own

✔ Create custom 3D assets that you can use in a mod and see your creations working in the game

✔ Optimize the geometry of your 3D models to perform their best when people use your mod

✔ Master exporting tools to get your content into GIANTS Editor and ultimately into the game

Chapter 6

Setting Up a Basic moddesc.xml

- -

In This Chapter

▶ Starting out with a new mod

▶ Giving your mod a title and description

▶ Making your mod available in the in-game store

▶ Setting up specializations

- -

*I*f you're making a mod, you're interested in having it played in-game. However, the game needs to be made aware of your mod's existence. Simply dropping it into Farming Simulator's mods folder isn't enough. Farming Simulator needs to know the name of your mod, what it is, if anything is special or unexpected about it, whether it works in multiplayer mode, and so on.

All of this information is included in a file, moddesc.xml. GIANTS Engine makes extensive use of the eXtensible Markup Language (XML) for configuration. In fact, the I3D format that GIANTS Editor uses is also based on XML.

All of the various rules and idiosyncrasies of XML are out of scope for this book. However, XML isn't that complex of a language once you start messing with it. You can find a decent primer on XML at w3schools (www.w3schools.com/xml/). However, because we're working on a file with a very specific means of formatting, you can just dive right in. I explain things along the way.

Creating a New modDesc.xml

Every mod has a `modDesc.xml` file, which means two things:

 ✔ Your mod needs to have a `modDesc.xml`.

 ✔ All other mods have a `modDesc.xml` that you can look at and use as a reference.

In fact, the nice folks at GIANTS Software have even included a sample mod with Farming Simulator, so you don't even need to go far to find an example. You can find it in the `sdk` folder where you have Farming Simulator installed (on Windows, it should be something like `C:\Program Files\Farming Simulator 2015\ sdk\sampleMod.zip`).

Looking at the file, notice the first line. It should look like this:

```
<?xml version="1.0" encoding="utf-8"
          standalone="no" ?>
```

Any `modDesc.xml` file (and really, any XML file in general) needs this as the first line. It lets anyone (and any program) reading the file know that this file is formatted in XML. The next line is where the mod actually starts:

```
<modDesc descVersion="20">
```

One of the defining attributes of XML is the tag. A *tag* is a segment of text, wrapped between less-than (<) and greater-than (>) symbols. The first word defines the type of tag. In this preceding example, you're looking at the `modDesc` open tag. All tags come in pairs: an *open* tag such as in the example, and a *close* tag, like this:

```
</modDesc>
```

A slash (/) as the first character indicates a close tag. Content, such as text or other tags that relate, appear between the open and close tags of a certain type (like this modDesc tag). Think of it as a means of categorizing. In this case, anything that falls between the open and close modDesc tags is information that describes a mod.

In addition to the content between open and close tags, an open tag can also have any number of *attributes.* In the case of the modDesc tag, there is a descVersion attribute, assigned the value of 20. Functionally, this just means that the format of modDesc.xml has been updated at least 20 times by GIANTS Software, and this particular file uses the twentieth version of the format. You should use the same attribute and value in your modDesc.xml.

Defining Mod Title and Descriptions

A set of tags used to name and describe your mod appears within the modDesc tag of your mod's modDesc.xml. The content of these tags doesn't show up in the in-game store, but GIANTS Engine still makes use of them. The following is a brief description of each tag.

- ✔ <author>: The person or group that created this mod. In this case, it should be your name.

- ✔ <version>: Assigning a version number to your mod is a good idea. When you release a mod, people have an expectation that you'll maintain it and fix any issues that users find with it. Having a version number is the easiest way to know if people are using the latest update of your mod or if they're using an old one.

- ✔ <title>: This is the name of your mod. You can *localize,* or translate, your mod's name for multiple languages. More on this in a bit.

✔ **<description>:** As you may expect, this tag is a short description of your mod. Like the title tag, you also can localize the description. It can be a just a few words or a length of sentences, although people tend to prefer brevity.

✔ **<iconFilename>:** You want your mod to be easily selected with an image, right? This tag is the path to an image (PNG or DDS) that serves as an icon for your mod. The image should be 256x256 pixels and, for simplicity, keep it in your mod's parent folder.

✔ **<multiplayer>:** This tag is a little bit strange because it doesn't appear to have an associated closing tag. It just has the supported attribute. Set this attribute to *true* if your mod is intended to work in multiplayer mode and *false* otherwise. As for closing the tag, have a look at the end of it and notice the slash (/) just before the greater-than (>) symbol. This is shorthand in XML for "There is no content to nest in this tag, just the attribute, so you can go ahead and close it here."

Allow me to pause a moment here and make a note about localization. Farming Simulator is a game that's enjoyed all over the world. In fact, it has been translated into 12 different languages. If you want your mod to work nicely for all these players, make the effort for it to appear in the player's preferred language.

To do so, localize the title and description. Just wrap the actual title or description in a set of tags defined by the two-letter designation for the language (for instance, *en* for English, *de* for German, *fr* for French, and so on). If you have another look at the sample mod that ships with Farming Simulator, you can see that its modDesc.xml is localized for English and German.

So if you've been building your custom modDesc.xml along with this text, you should have something that looks similar to the following:

```
<?xml version="1.0" encoding="utf-8"
          standalone="no" ?>
<modDesc descVersion="20">
  <author>My Name</author>
  <version>1.0</version>
  <title>
    <en>My Mod</en>
    <de>Mein Mod</de>
  </title>
  <description>
    <en>My mod description</en>
    <de>Meine Mod Beschreibung</de>
  </description>
  <iconFilename>modIcon.dds</iconFilename>
  <multiplayer supported="true"/>
</modDesc>
```

This is a start, but it's not the whole story. GIANTS Engine
may be aware of your mod, but without adding it to the
in-game store, the player has no idea it's there. The next
section of this chapter covers that topic.

Adding In-Game Store Items

You have your modDesc.xml file half-created. You just
need to make your mod visible to the in-game store,
which is why the storeItems section of the file exists.
Typically, the convention is to put the storeItems tag
just after multiplayer. Note that this tag is storeItems,
plural. You can nest another tag, storeItems, within the
storeItems section in order to have a mod that adds
multiple items to the store. For simplicity's sake, however,
assume for the time being that your mod only adds a
single item to the store. In that case, quite a bit of the information you've already typed in the beginning of modDesc.
xml is repeated within the storeItems section.

The first two tags of note in the storeItems section
are name and functions. Generally speaking, you want
to use the same basic information here that you use in

the first half of your modDesc.xml (refer to the previous section in this chapter), though you have a greater opportunity to have a longer description for the store. That said, the storeItems section has two major differences pertaining to the name and functions tags when compared to the title and functions tags in the upper half:

- ✔ **Localization:** Whereas in the first part of modDesc.xml, you have localized versions *within* the title and functions tags, the name and functions tags in the storeItems section are localized together; the language tags (such as *en, de, fr,* and so on) are parent sections that name and functions tags for each language are nested into.

- ✔ **CDATA functions:** This one has the real potential for throwing you off. The functions in the storeItems section all appear to be wrapped in a strange tag that starts with <![CDATA[and ends with]]>. This just means that the text between those square brackets should be considered *character data,* which means that you can interpret this text as XML, but the XML reader shouldn't.

Beyond the name and functions tags, you need to include a handful of other tags in the storeItems section:

- ✔ **<rotation>:** The rotation of your mod when it's bought and inserted in the game. For consistency with other mods, try to keep this at 0.

- ✔ **<image>:** This tag is like the multiplayer tag in that it's self-closing and only has attributes. In fact, it has two:

  - • **active:** This is the path to an image you want to use as your mod's icon in the store. It should be exactly the same as the image in the iconFilename tag. Even if it's not the same file, it should follow the same rules (256x256 pixels, PNG or DDS format – DDS is preferred).

- **brand:** Often a mod will be a known vehicle of a known brand. This attribute points to an image (256x128 pixels, PNG or DDS format — DDS is preferred) that represents that brand.

✔ **<price>:** This is the amount of in-game money you expect the player to spend on purchasing your mod.

✔ **<dailyUpkeep>:** This is the amount of daily in-game money that a player must spend to keep your mod on his or her farm.

✔ **<xmlFilename>:** Complex mods, such as vehicles, have their own XML file that defines additional attributes (see Chapter 11 for more details). This tag is the path to that XML file. If you're being properly organized, this file should be in the same folder as your modDesc.xml.

✔ **<brand>:** If your mod is of a specific brand, you can include it here. If that brand is already used in the game, you can use Farming Simulator's variable name for it (this is why the brand tag in the provided sample mod starts with a dollar symbol). You can also put any other brand name you want here.

✔ **<category>:** If your mod is a machine or vehicle, you need to specify a type. The following lists all of the available machine types you can choose.

• baling	• potatoHarvesting
• beetHarvesting	• slurryTanks
• cultivators	• sowingMachines
• feeding	• sprayers
• fertilerSpreaders	• tedders
• frontLoaders	• tippers
• harvesters	• tractors
• loaderWagons	• weights
• manureSpreaders	• windrowers
• mowers	• woodShredder
• plows	• misc

At this point, your full `modDesc.xml` should look akin to the following:

```xml
<?xml version="1.0" encoding="utf-8"
        standalone="no" ?>
<modDesc descVersion="20">
  <author>My Name</author>
  <version>1.0</version>
  <title>
    <en>My Mod</en>
    <de>Mein Mod</de>
  </title>
  <functions>
    <function> $l10n_function_plough
        </function>
  </functions>
  <iconFilename>modIcon.dds</iconFilename>
  <multiplayer supported="true"/>
  <storeItems>
    <storeItem>
      <en>
        <name>My Mod</name>
        <functions>
<function>$l10n_function_plough</function>
        </functions>
      </en>
      <de>
        <name>Mein Mod</name>
        <description>
<![CDATA[Dies ist der Beispielmod.]]>
        </description>
      </de>
      <rotation>0</rotation>
      <image active="modIcon.dds"
          brand="brand.dds"/>
      <price>1995</price>
      <dailyUpkeep>85</dailyUpkeep>
      <xmlFilename>mod.xml</xmlFilename>
      <brand>my_brand</brand>
      <category>plows</category>
    </storeItem>
  </storeItems>
</modDesc>
```

For the most part, that's it. You should have enough to get started. Some specific tags are relevant if your mod is a map or does something really different. However, if you have a mod, you can easily find a mod that does something at least a little bit similar and look at its modDesc. xml for pointers on how to properly format yours.

Including Specializations

You need some way to let GIANTS Engine and Farming Simulator know about your new and awesome mod. Of course, the way to do that is through the modDesc.xml file with something known as a specialization.

In Farming Simulator, a *specialization* is a specific functionality or feature that you've included in your tractor or other modified machinery. Default specializations include steerable, sprayer, or baler. For a more comprehensive list of default specializations, have a look at the Farming Simulator script documentation online at www.ls-mods. de/scriptDocumentation.php. Almost 90 different specializations are defined there.

A vehicle can actually have multiple specializations, such as having an attachable sprayer and being steerable. And, of course, you can also define your own specializations with a Lua script.

Adding specializations to your modDesc.xml is pretty simple. You only point to the external specialization scripts that you need. By convention, most modders add mark-up for specializations just before the storeItems tag.

To include one of the default specializations that ship with Farming Simulator, you need to first add a section in your modDesc.xml called vehicleTypes. Within the vehicleTypes section, you specify a type and its specialization. For example, say your mod has a steerable

specialization. The code you add would look something
like the following

```
<vehicleTypes>
    <type name="myMod" className="Vehicle"
            filename=$dataS/scripts/
            vehicles/Vehicle.lua">
        <specialization name="steerable" />
    </type>
</vehicleTypes>
```

In this mark-up, the `type` tag takes up the most space.
The following is a description of its attributes:

- ✔ **name:** The name of your mod, or more specifically,
  the vehicle or machine in your mod.

- ✔ **className:** This reflects the vehicle class that your
  mod belongs to. All of the default vehicles, for example, are in the Vehicle class. Writing your own class
  in Lua is possible but usually not necessary.

- ✔ **filename:** This may look a touch odd to you.
  The fact that it starts with a dollar sign ($) means
  that this variable is internal to Farming Simulator.
  In the example, it points to the main Lua script
  that defines vehicles. Don't go looking for that
  script on your hard drive, though. It's archived
  within a file.

A specialization tag with a single attribute, `name`, is
within the open and close `type` tags. This is the name
of the default specialization you wish to include with
your mod.

If you want to include multiple default specializations on your mod, you only need to include more
`specialization` tags within the `type` section.
However, you don't need more than one `type` section unless your mod includes multiple machines
or vehicles.

Chapter 7

Making a New 3D Mod

In This Chapter

▶ Creating a mod template

▶ Organizing your mod within your 3D program

▶ Preparing for textures

▶ Optimizing your model

*Y*ou technically can build a Farming Simulator mod using only GIANTS Editor and a text editor like Notepad++. In fact, you can make a mod using just the text editor. However, I certainly don't recommend it. 3D programs for digital content creation (DCC) such as Blender, Maya, and 3ds Max are way faster and offer a wide array of modeling, texturing, and animation tools that make a modder's life much more pleasant.

That said, these 3D DCC programs are typically quite complex in their own rights, and it takes time and effort to gain mastery over any of them. This chapter focuses solely on the best practices for using 3D DCC tools in creating mods. If you're not familiar with Blender, Maya, or 3ds Max, then you may need to do some reading on your own. Fortunately, many helpful resources and tutorials are available on the Internet as well as books on these programs.

Of the different 3D programs, Blender is by far the most accessible, largely because it's free. Because it is free (and maybe a little because I'm a Blender guy at heart), most of the examples and screenshots in this chapter are from Blender. However, if you're familiar with another 3D program, the same basic principles should apply.

Setting Up a New Scene

If you make a lot of mods, you can find yourself spending a lot of time just setting up a scene and configuring some basic settings each time. Rather than go through these steps over and over again, I suggest that you create a template project, which is a baseline file that has all of those basic things already set up for you. That way, you just need to launch your 3D DCC tool and jump right in.

In Blender, you should make a few changes to the default scene right off the bat:

- ✔ **Delete everything.** Blender's default scene is a lamp, a camera, and a cube object. Select them all (A) and delete them. The default point lamp isn't a good representation of the world light in Farming Simulator and you only need cameras for vehicle mods. Although the cube is a great starting point for modeling, deleting it now and adding it back later if you need it is faster.

- ✔ **Use real-world units.** In Scene Properties, expand the Units panel and change the Units setting from None to either Metric or Imperial. Doing so isn't absolutely required because the I3D exporter treats one Blender unit as one meter, but doing so is helpful for keeping units in mind while working. This is especially true if you happen to live in a part of the world that hasn't fully converted to metric.

- ✔ **Set Blender Internal as your default renderer.** This setting is already the default in Blender, but many Blender users often change this default to Blender's other renderer, Cycles. Cycles is a great renderer, but with it selected, getting a good idea of what your mod will look like in-game is much more difficult.

- ✔ **Enable GLSL shading and Backface Culling.** In the Properties region of the 3D View (the *N panel*), go to the Shading panel and change the Material Mode drop-down menu from Multitexture to GLSL. (*Note:* If you don't have Blender Internal set as your renderer, you won't see this option.) With these set, you can get a good idea of the in-game appearance of your model when you have the 3D View set for textured shading (Alt+Z).

✔ **Add a Sun lamp on layer 20.** More than likely you won't want to export this lamp with your model for the game. However, you need some kind of light in your scene so you can see what your mod looks like with textured shading (otherwise, it's just a big black blob) and the Sun lamp is a decent approximation of Farming Simulator's world light. By putting the lamp on layer 20, you can quickly toggle it on and off by enabling and disabling that layer.

After you make these changes, save your file (File➪Save As or Shift+Ctrl+S) to a place you can remember with a name that makes sense, like `mod_template.blend`.

Depending on your computer hardware, you may also want to set a user setting for performance reasons. If you have a relatively modern video card, you should set Blender to use vertex buffer objects (VBOs), a more efficient way of managing data in the 3D View, especially in large scenes or in models with a lot of vertices. To enable VBOs, open User Preferences (Ctrl+Alt+U) and go to the System section. You can find a small checkbox labeled VBOs in the middle of the center column (refer to Figure 7-1).

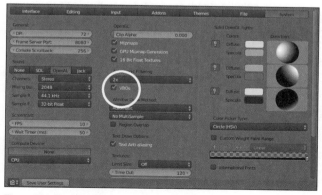

Figure 7-1: Enable VBOs in User Preferences.

Click the VBOs checkbox to enable them and then click the Save User Settings button at the bottom left of the window so VBOs are enabled every time you open Blender.

One of the key differences between Blender and GIANTS Editor is the world orientation. GIANTS Editor (along with a number of other common 3D DCC programs) has a *y-up world,* meaning the *y*-axis is the vertical axis while the *x*- and *z*-axes form the ground plane. Blender's world, on the other hand, is *z*-up. So in Blender, the ground is defined by the *x*- and *y*-axes while the *z*-axis is the vertical one. It's not as disorienting as it sounds, but sometimes it takes people a while to get used to it.

Establishing Object Hierarchy

From working with the Scenegraph in GIANTS Editor, you know the importance of having a clear object hierarchy with your mod. That means objects in your model should be organized via parent-child relationships. For example, if you're working on a vehicle mod, then all of the various parts of your vehicle — the wheels, windows, lights, cameras, and so forth — should be the child of a single, selectable object with the name of your vehicle.

Getting it right in your 3D DCC is important because of a direct correlation between the hierarchy you set up and the one that you end up with in GIANTS Editor. Figure 7-2 shows the Outliner in Blender for a properly configured model and the resulting Scenegraph in GIANTS Editor after exporting.

Figure 7-2: The Blender Outliner (left) and the GIANTS Editor Scenegraph after exporting (right).

When setting up your hierarchy, keep in mind these basic best practices:

✓ Use empties as makeshift transform groups.
Blender's grouping feature is completely different from the one GIANTS Editor uses and therefore doesn't translate nicely upon export. Instead, when you want a transform group, add an empty object in Blender and the parent of all the objects you want in that group (select the child objects, select your empty, and press Ctrl+P). The I3D exporter will correctly interpret this as a transform group.

✓ **Name everything.** All of the names you use in
   Blender are used when exported to I3D. You can
   easily get confused if you look in the Scenegraph
   and see all of your objects named some variation
   of Cube.023. Furthermore, stick with conventions
   used in GIANTS Editor. Basic conventions are as
   follows:

   • Main name is in camel case (such as
      frontLightSpot).

   • Use _col as a suffix for collision objects (for
      instance, wheelLeftBack_col).

   • Use _vis as a suffix for visualization objects,
      such as the textured mesh of your model or
      your light cones, used in-game (for instance,
      myMod_vis).

   • Numerically prefix your primary mesh elements,
      the immediate children of your parent object,
      as *XX*, where *XX* is some number (for example
      _05_indoorCamera).

✓ **The parent object for your vehicle should be a
   low-resolution mesh.** Use something that's 20–40 triangles, which works as a rough collision mesh. Let
   the high-resolution, textured visualization mesh be
   an unnumbered child of this mesh. It should share
   the same name, but have the _vis suffix.

Configuring Materials and Textures

The general rule for Farming Simulator mods is that a
single object mod such as a vehicle, trailer, or building,
should only have one material. As a result, if your object
is composed of multiple separated parts, they all have
to share the same material settings. You may then ask,
"Then how do you make parts of your model different
colors?" The answer: textures. As Chapter 3 explains, an
object's material can have up to three different textures:

- ✓ **Diffuse:** The base colors for your model.

- ✓ **Specular:** A grayscale image that controls the shininess of the material.

- ✓ **Normal:** A kind of wacky color image that helps make your model look like it has more detail than is really there.

Chapter 9 discusses in greater depth the creation of these textures. This section specifically relates to setting up your base material and preparing your 3D model for receiving textures. Going with one material is the general rule with a few exceptions:

- ✓ **Wheels:** If you're making a vehicle mod, your vehicle's wheels can have a separate material. Note that all of the wheels must share the same material, but it can be different from the main vehicle's material.

- ✓ **Windows:** Windows in a vehicle may also have a separate material. The caveat: All glass elements should be joined as a single object (select all glass objects in Blender and press Ctrl+J) and shouldn't have any textures for normal maps or specular maps.

- ✓ **Light glow (corona):** For the glow of that shines around lights when they're turned on, you should use flat planes with a single diffuse texture.

Just like the objects in your mod, make sure you name your materials something logical. Also, the convention in GIANTS Editor is to add _mat as a suffix to the material name (for example, hugeWoodenBarn_mat). For a single mod, it may not seem like that big of a deal, but it's a good habit to get into. That way, if you find yourself making a big mod, you already have good habits and your files will be nicely organized and easy to maintain.

Defining material settings

Setting up a material for your mod in Blender is remark-
ably easy. For the most part, you stick with the default
settings for the following on your mod:

Main materials

For your mod's main material, the standard Lambert
diffuse shader and Cook-Torrance (CookTorr) specular
shaders work just fine. If your mod has a more metal-like
surface, you may want to dial down the Hardness value
on the specular shader. The default is 50, which is a bit
plastic looking; setting it to 25 works nicely.

Change the name of your material from Material to something that makes more sense, like myVehicleMod_mat.
That's basically it. The only other thing you should do is
make sure that each of the subobjects in your mod are also
using the same material datablock. The *user count* for your
material (the number next to your material's name in the
data block selector of Material Properties) should equal the
number of objects in your mod that aren't wheels, windows,
or coronas.

Wheels

The material for your wheels should be roughly the same
as your main material. You may want to turn down the
hardness in the specular shader even more (like around 20)
because tires typically aren't shiny unless they're polished
for being displayed on a showroom floor. Again, name your
material something logical, like wheels_mat and make
sure all of your wheel objects use this material.

Windows

The settings for your window material require a little bit
more tweaking. Starting with the default material, you
need to make a couple changes:

 ✔ Set the specular color to black.

 ✔ Enable the checkbox for the Transparency panel.

You may be tempted to play with the Alpha value in the Transparency panel or shift the hue on the diffuse color to be slightly bluer. Don't. You can set both of them with a texture very quickly. And unlike the main material and your wheels material, your window material (properly named, like `window_mat`) should only be assigned to one object. All glass meshes should be joined (Ctrl+J) into this single object.

Corona materials

For corona materials, start with the same settings your window material has and then add a few things, such as:

✔ Enable the Shadeless checkbox in the Shading panel.

✔ In the Custom Properties panel, add a new property called `customShader` with a value of `emissive BillboardShader.xml`. The I3D exporter uses this custom property. You just need to make sure you have that particular XML file in the same folder as your mod.

You can get the `emissiveBillboardShader.xml` file from the sample mod that comes in the `sdk` folder where Farming Simulator is installed on your computer.

Unwrapping objects for texturing

Before you can texture your model, you need to unwrap your mesh. *Unwrapping* is the process used to map a pixel's location on the image to a corresponding location on the mesh in 3D space using *UV coordinates*. Imagine taking your mesh's surface, flattening it out, and positioning the pattern of that flat chunk on a canvas you plan on painting. That pattern defines your UV coordinates.

To understand unwrapping, think about how mapmakers make world maps. Longitude and latitude lines form a grid (a mesh, if you will) around the globe's surface. You can then define one or more of those lines as *seams,* along which you can split the surface and flatten it to a map. Cartographers were the world's first 3D texture artists!

In Blender, unwrapping a single object is really quite easy. To make your life easier, you may want to switch screen layouts to the UV Editing screen. You can quickly get there from the Default screen by pressing Ctrl+Right Arrow four times, or you can use the Screen layout drop-down menu at the top of the Blender window. Do so and you should see something similar to Figure 7-3.

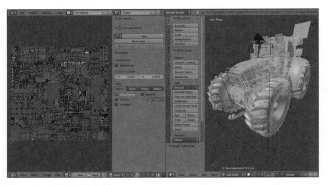

Figure 7-3: The UV Editing screen layout in Blender is great for unwrapping meshes.

To begin unwrapping your mesh, use the following steps:

1. **Select the object you wish to unwrap.**

2. **Toggle into Edit mode (Tab).**

3. **Switch into Edge Select (Ctrl+Tab⇨Edge).**

4. **Select the edge or edges you want to be treated as seams.**

5. **Mark the selected edges as seams (Ctrl+E⇨Mark Seam).**

6. **Select all (press A until everything is selected).**

7. Unwrap your object (U➪Unwrap).

8. Tweak the UV layout in the UV/Image Editor to make the most use of the available space without allowing for any overlaps.

You may need to repeat Steps 5–8 a couple times to get the layout you like. When you're done, you may have something like Figure 7-4.

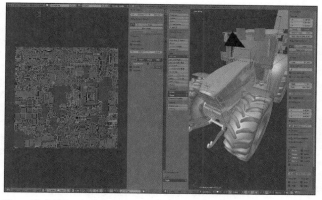

Figure 7-4: The results of unwrapping an object in Blender.

Unwrapping in Blender does have one complication. Blender currently doesn't have a nice way to unwrap multiple objects at the same time. Because most of your objects in your mod have to share the same material, it means they also must share the same texture. So the UV coordinates for each object have to be arranged in a single layout without overlapping. But because Blender can't have more than one object in Edit mode at the same time, there's no clean way to see or edit the UV coordinates of all objects at once.

The easiest way to do it is to join all of your meshes into a single object like you do for the windows. This solution is the quickest and easiest. If you need objects to be separate in GIANTS Editor for specializations or animation, you can always reseparate them after you unwrap. Doing so only gets complicated if you've used a lot of modifiers to create the various objects in your mod. You'll need to apply those modifiers prior to joining, which is fine if unwrapping is the last step in your process, but it may make it difficult to edit your object later.

Using Your Triangles Effectively

GIANTS Engine, like all game engines, must perform in *real time*. That is, the game engine needs to update the 3D assets on your computer monitor fast enough so changes appear to be happening immediately. If a player presses a control to move the main character, that character needs to walk as directed, and the 3D environment needs to update as the character moves around. As you may imagine, this demands a lot of processing power from your computer's hardware. The more geometry on-screen means the harder the computer has to work and the greater the likelihood that the player may notice lagging or glitches in the game.

As a modder, your job is to help the game engine avoid having any of those lags or glitches. A major way to do so is by optimizing your 3D models to only use as much geometry — vertices and triangles — as is absolutely necessary. And if you can get away with it, use *less than* what's necessary and fake the details as much as possible.

When it comes to 3D graphics, one of the things that I regularly tell people is, "If you're not faking it, then you're probably doing it wrong." These sections share tricks for faking it right to keep the game engine fast and happy.

Getting your normals right

A common problem many first-time 3D modelers make is their normals sometimes face the wrong way. A *normal* is an imaginary line that points orthogonally, or perpendicularly, to a polygon. A game engine's renderer uses normals to calculate how light reacts to the surface of a mesh, thereby determining where highlights and shadows fall. The catch, however, is that a normal only points away from one side of a polygon. The backside of the polygon (the side without the normal) often shows up in a game engine with improper lighting . . . if it shows up at all!

For this reason, make sure that the normals on the polygons of your 3D model all face outward. Blender has a convenient shortcut that does it for you very quickly. From Edit mode, simply select all of the polygons in your mesh (A) and then press Ctrl+N (or Mesh⇨Normals⇨Recalculate Outside from the menu).

If this doesn't fix the issue, chances are good that your model has some unconventional things happening in the mesh, such as interior faces or doubled-up geometry.

Reducing polygon count

To have a lower number of polygons, you first need to know how many you have. In Blender, the Info editor's header that's typically at the top of the window constantly gives you an accurate count of the geometry in the scene. Figure 7-5 shows an example of this data in Blender's interface.

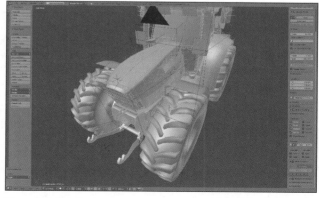

Figure 7-5: Blender keeps an accurate accounting of the geometry in your scene.

The most important number in this series is the one after the word *Tris,* for triangles, which is 20,566 in Figure 7-5. The reason why you're only interested in triangles is because in GIANTS Engine, like in most game engines, all geometry is ultimately converted into triangles. And for a mod, you want to pay attention to the total triangle count for all of the objects in that mod.

When you have an object in Edit mode, the information in the Info editor's header only shows information relevant to the active object.

GIANTS Software has a set of recommended *triangle budgets,* or the maximum recommended number of triangles for different kinds of mods. Table 7-1 lists the triangle budgets for the three main kinds of mods.

Table 7-1   Triangle Budgets for the Main Types of Vehicles

Mod Type	Triangle Budget
Bins/Trailers	15,000 triangles
Tractors	25,000 triangles
Large machinery (such as combine harvesters)	50,000 triangles

You can use several different tricks for reducing the number of triangles in your model. The following are a set of guidelines and recommendations you can use for keeping that count down:

✔ **Merge polygons in flat areas to a few large polygons.** In general, this act reduces the total triangle count when the polygons get converted.

✔ **Avoid *n-gons*, or polygons with more than four sides, in your final model.** N-gons are great for making the modeling process efficient, but every game engine converts them to triangles differently. Do that conversion upfront to avoid unexpected visual glitches.

✔ **Use sharp edge markers (Ctrl+E⇨Mark Sharp in Edit mode) and the Edge Split modifier rather than adding extra geometry to get hard edges.** This method gives your model sharp edges without increasing your triangle count.

✔ **Avoid modifiers that add geometry like the Subdivision Surface and Bevel modifiers.** These modifiers can make your model look really nice, but they can also spike your triangle count, often quite substantially, which you want to avoid.

✔ **Use linked duplicates where possible.** If you duplicate an object using linked duplicates (other programs may call them *clones* or *instances*), you have multiple objects that share the same mesh data. This doesn't really reduce the raw polygon count (even duplicated triangles need to be processed and rendered), but linked duplicates are more efficient, and most game engines are optimized to take advantage of them. Besides, linked duplicates make modeling changes on all of those duplicates faster, too.

✔ **Use the Decimate modifier.** This modifier is really a measure of last resort. It's quite powerful, especially using the Un-Subdivide setting. However, the control you have over this modifier is limited and you may end up spending a lot of time cleaning up your geometry after applying this modifier.

✔ **Model/Sculpt in high detail and bake those details into normal map.** A normal map can fake the appearance of more detailed geometry when applied to a mesh with less-dense geometry.

Generating normal maps for additional detail

Making 3D models for video games puts a digital artist at cross-purposes. You know that increased detail on your model helps a player get more immersed in the game. However, you also know that excessive detail can get computationally expensive, potentially making the game unplayable.

You can fake it a bit by painting some details in the diffuse texture, but some of those details won't look right. It looks painted on, like headlight stickers on a racecar. The light in the scene simply doesn't react correctly. Having texture that makes light react as if there are surface variations in your mesh even when they're not really there would be nice. This, in essence, is what a normal map does.

A *normal map* is a 2D image wherein the colors of the image tell the game engine's renderer that light should bounce off of the mesh's surface in a specific direction other than the default. With it, you can fake detailed, dynamic shadows and highlights on a relatively simple mesh. Although digitally painting a normal map by hand is completely possible, doing so is a lot of work and can get confusing pretty quickly. Baking a normal map is a better, less painful way to do it. *Baking* basically involves using the geometry of one mesh with a lot of detail and geometry and comparing it to another mesh with much fewer triangles. The difference between those two meshes is encoded, or baked, to a 2D image according to the UV layout of the low-detail model.

Some artists prefer to start with the high-resolution model. They go gung-ho and model in as much detail as they can muster. Then they take that high-resolution model and *retopologize* it, or create another model of lower resolution using the high-resolution model as a guide. Sometimes they use shortcuts, such as Blender's Decimate modifier or the Shrinkwrap modifier. More often than not, however, it involves rebuilding the model one vertex at a time.

Another set of artists is on the opposite end of the spectrum. These artists prefer to start with the low-resolution mesh. They keep that mesh as a base and either duplicate it or add a Multiresolution modifier. Then they use sculpting and modeling tools to create the high-resolution details on top of that base.

Regardless of the technique you choose (try them both, it's really a matter of taste and determining which is most right for you), you typically end up with two meshes, a high-resolution one with a lot of detail and a low-resolution one that you intend to use in-game. After you have these two meshes, then in Blender, the baking process uses the following steps:

1. **Make sure your low-resolution object is UV unwrapped.**

   You're ultimately going to load this object into GIANTS Editor.

2. **Select the low-resolution mesh and toggle into Edit mode (Tab).**

3. **From the UV/Image Editor, add a new blank image.**

   The size of the image depends on the size of your object. Small objects get small sizes whereas large objects get larger sizes. Bear in mind that this image should follow the same texture size rules described in Chapter 9. The width and height must be numbers that are a power of two and neither can be larger than 2,048 pixels.

4. **Toggle back into Object mode.**

5. **Select your high-resolution mesh and Shift+Select your low-resolution mesh.**

   Order is very important here, so make sure you pick your low-resolution mesh last so it is the active object. Also, you want both meshes to be in the exact same spot; they should overlap one another.

6. **In Render Properties, within the Bake panel, use the following settings:**

   • Choose Normals from the Bake Mode drop-down menu.

   • Ensure that Tangent is picked from the Normal Space drop-down menu.

   • Enable the Selected to Active checkbox. This checkbox is particularly important because it's a core part of what makes the next step work.

7. **Click the Bake button.**

   In the UV/Image Editor, you should see the black, blank image fill in with a bluish image. This image is your normal map.

8. **Save the normal map to your hard drive using the GIANTS texture-naming convention.**

   For example, myMod_normal.png

Now that you have your normal map generated, you can include it with your low-resolution mesh's textures as part of its material. Refer to Chapter 9 for more on this step.

If your mod consists of multiple objects, you're going to run into a similar situation as with materials. You need to bake each object to the same image texture, which means that you need to bake new data without overwriting your previous bakes. To do so, disable the Clear checkbox in the Bake panel of Render Properties. Alternatively, you can bake to multiple images and combine them into a single image using Photoshop.

Chapter 8

Exporting Your Mod for GIANTS Editor

● ●

In This Chapter

▶ Getting 3D content out of Blender

▶ Pushing your model out from Maya

▶ Moving your mod from 3ds Max to GIANTS Editor

▶ Using FBX instead of I3D

▶ Pulling your mod into GIANTS Editor

● ●

*Y*ou're ready to get your model in GIANTS Editor so you can include it with your mod, and ultimately play with it in Farming Simulator. What you need is the ability to export that model in a format that GIANTS Editor understands, either I3D or FBX. Farming Simulator includes some exporter plugins for three of the main 3D suites used by modders: Blender, Maya, and 3ds Max. You can find them in the sdk folder where you've installed Farming Simulator (on Windows, this is something like C:\Program Files\Farming Simulator 2015\sdk).

This chapter walks you through exporting your model from these programs into a format usable by GIANTS Engine.

Despite the fact that those exporter plugins come with Farming Simulator, you should also look at the GIANTS Developer Network (GDN) website (http://gdn. giants-software.com). You can usually find more updated versions of the exporter plugins than the ones that ship with Farming Simulator.

Exporting from Blender

Blender is my favorite 3D content creation program. It's very powerful, lightweight, free, and open source. If you're just getting started with modding, Blender is a low-cost way to get your feet wet without being concerned that you'll blow through a 30-day free trial period. I am immensely pleased to know that GIANTS Software maintains an I3D exporter add-on for Blender.

These sections give you the lowdown on just what you need to know when exporting your mods from Blender.

Installing the I3D exporter add-on

An installer simplifies the process of getting the add-on to appear in Blender. You just run the installer executable, assuming you're using Windows. You can find the installer in the sdk folder where Farming Simulator is installed on your computer (or your Downloads folder if you have the latest version from the GDN). The filename of the installer should be something like blender_i3d_ export_6.0.0.exe. Figure 8-1 shows what it looks like when you run it.

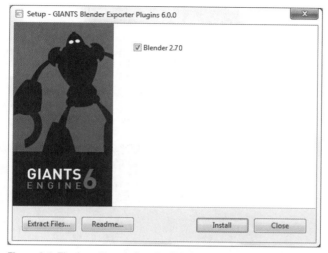

Figure 8-1: The installer window for GIANTS Blender exporter plugins.

If the installer can find where you have Blender installed, it shows it as a checkbox option in the installer window. If you have multiple versions of Blender installed, you can even pick which ones you want to install the add-on. Click the Install button and when the installer finishes, it pops up a dialog to let you know installation was successful, as Figure 8-2 shows.

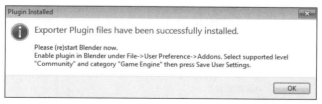

Figure 8-2: When the installer successfully completes, a confirmation dialog pops up with additional instructions.

To enable the add-on within Blender, start Blender and
go to User Preferences (File⇨User Preferences or use
the Ctrl+Alt+U hotkey combination). In the Addons section, go to the Game Engine category. You should see an
add-on named GIANTS I3D Exporter Tools. Click the tri-
angular icon to the left of the name to expand it and see
more information about the add-on, including buttons for
documentation and bug reporting. You should see something similar to Figure 8-3.

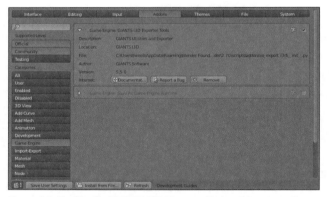

Figure 8-3: Enable the GIANTS I3D Exporter Tools add-on from User
Preferences in Blender.

Enable the GIANTS I3D Exporter Tools add-on by clicking the checkbox to the far right of its name in User
Preferences. For convenience, you may also want to
click the Save User Settings button at the lower left of
User Preferences. That way, the add-on is automatically
enabled whenever you start Blender and you don't have
to manually enable the add-on every time you want to
use it.

Manually installing in Blender

Because Blender is open source, you have more than one way to run it on a computer. In fact, you don't even need to have Blender installed at all. For example, I have a copy of Blender on a USB stick that I carry around with me wherever I go, so I can use Blender on any computer. Fortunately, the installer for the Blender I3D exporter add-on accounts for Blender's flexibility.

If you run the installer and it can't find Blender installed in the expected path, you have the option of manually extracting the add-on's files by clicking the Extract Files button in the lower-left corner (refer to Figure 8-1). Pay attention to where you're extracting those files on your hard drive. A quick place to extract is on your desktop.

After you extract the files, start Blender and open User Preferences (File⇨User Preferences or Ctrl+Alt+U). Go to the Addons section and click the Install from File button at the bottom of the window. Then, using the File Browser, navigate to the extracted files and choose the io_export_i3d.zip file. After doing so, you should see the GIANTS I3D Exporter Tools add-on available in the Game Engine category, like in Figure 8-3. Then you can enable the add-on like you would any other add-on in Blender (click the checkbox to the right of the add-on's name).

Exporting your mod

With the GIANTS I3D Exporter Tools add-on installed and enabled in Blender, you can finally get your scene ready for GIANTS Editor. The GIANTS exporter is very different from most exporters in Blender. It doesn't appear in the File⇨Export menu. Instead, look to the far right of the Info editor's header (typically at the top of the Blender window) to see the text that reads GIANTS I3D. Click that text and click I3D Exporter from the menu that appears. In the 3D View's Properties region, a GIANTS I3D Exporter panel appears. There are two subsections:

✔ **Export:** The subpanels in the Export section contain options relevant to the overall export process, including the ability to choose the types of objects to export and your export filename.

✔ **Attributes:** The Attributes section gives a series of options pertaining to the current active object, much like the Attributes panel in GIANTS Editor.

Figure 8-4 shows the options available in the GIANTS I3D Exporter panel.

Figure 8-4: Clicking the GIANTS I3D button reveals the GIANTS I3D Exporter panel in the 3D View's Properties region.

For the most part, you should be fine with the default settings. At the bottom of the Export section are two buttons: Export All and Export Selected. The former exports your whole Blender scene into an I3D file, whereas the latter only exports the current selected objects. In either case, the default behavior exports to an I3D file that shares the same name as your .blend file.

The Blender exporter add-on doesn't currently support all the features of the I3D format. Animations and vertex weighting, in particular, don't currently work.

Exporting from Maya

Autodesk's Maya is probably the most commonly used 3D digital content creation (DCC) tool in the video game industry at this time. The price tag can be a bit steep for an independent mod maker, but it's certainly the go-to tool for many professional 3D artists. You can try it with a 30-day trial that you can download from Autodesk's website.

If you use Maya, the following sections walk you through what you need to know to install and use the Maya I3D exporter plugin.

Installing the I3D exporter plugin

Installing the Maya I3D exporter plugin is a simple process. An installer handles the whole thing for you.

You can find the installer in the `sdk` folder where Farming Simulator is installed on your computer (or your Downloads folder if you got the latest version from the GDN). The filename of the installer should be something like `maya_i3d_export_6.0.0.exe`. When you run it, you should get a window like the one in Figure 8-5.

The installer should be able to detect where you have Maya installed on your computer and offer a checkbox for that location. Assuming it's correct, click the Install button.

Figure 8-5: The installer window for GIANTS Maya exporter plugin.

After the installer finishes, start (or restart) Maya. You should notice a custom shelf named GIANTS. In that shelf is an icon for GIANTS I3D Tools, as shown in Figure 8-6.

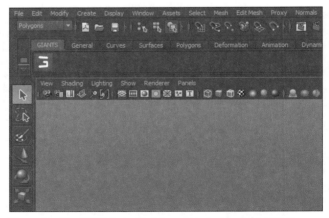

Figure 8-6: The GIANTS shelf in Maya with the icon for GIANTS I3D Tools.

Note that in Figure 8-6, the shelf has been shifted to the far left. When first installed, the GIANTS shelf appears on the far right after Maya's Custom shelf.

Exporting your mod

To export your mod from Maya so that GIANTS Editor can load it, click the GIANTS I3D Tools icon in the GIANTS shelf. This brings up the GIANTS I3D Tools dialog, as shown in Figure 8-7.

Figure 8-7: The GIANTS I3D Tools dialog is where you go to export your 3D objects for your mod.

You may notice a *lot* of options and settings, spread across four different tabs. Going through these options at great detail is outside the scope of this book. However, generally speaking, you can leave all options at their default values. You absolutely must make one change, which is in the Output File section of the Export tab. You need to set the File Location, which is the location on your hard drive where the exporter puts the I3D file. You manually can type in that path, but the easier way is to click the folder icon to the right of the File Location text field and use the file browser to specify where the file goes. Typically, this location is the folder where your mod is.

With the File Location set, just click the Export All button and the whole scene is exported as an I3D file that you can open in GIANTS Editor.

Exporting from 3ds Max

3ds Max is the old standby of 3D digital content creation (DCC) for video games. Though its popularity has waned a bit in recent years, Autodesk's old soldier still commands an impressive segment of the professional DCC market, especially as it pertains to the video game industry.

It's a bit costly for independent and hobbyist modders, but if you have a license for 3ds Max, you can't go wrong with it. You can download a 30-day trial from Autodesk's website if you want to test it. These sections take a closer look at using 3ds Max when exporting your mods.

Installing the I3D exporter plugin

GIANTS Software has an installer that dramatically simplifies the process of getting the I3D exporter plugin to work in 3ds Max. You can find the installer in the sdk folder where Farming Simulator is installed on your computer (or your Downloads folder if you got the latest version from the GDN). The file name of the installer should be something like max_i3d_export_6.0.0.exe. When you run it, you should get a window like the one in Figure 8-8.

Figure 8-8: The installer window for GIANTS 3ds Max exporter plugins.

The installer should be able to find where you've installed 3ds Max on your computer and provide a checkbox to ensure that's where you want the plugin to go. Click the Install button. When the installation is complete, you can start or restart 3ds Max to use the exporter.

Exporting your mod

The exporting process for 3ds Max is very straightforward. Click on the Max button in the upper-right corner of the window and go to the Export menu item. You can either export the whole scene or just export the current selection. Which one you choose depends mostly on the nature of your mod. If you're not sure, just choose to export the whole scene.

After you click Export, 3ds Max produces a file browser dialog for you to pick where on your hard drive your scene should be exported. Navigate to the folder of your custom mod and type in a name for your file. *Remember:* You need to choose the GIANTS I3D (*.I3D) option from the Save as type drop-down menu. Figure 8-9 shows what your file browser dialog should look like in 3ds Max.

Figure 8-9: Choose the GIANTS I3D (*.I3D) option from the Save as type drop-down menu.

After you pick where to export and set the file type to I3D, click the Save button. Another dialog opens with a series of options for controlling how your scene is exported. In the simplest cases, you can keep all options at their default values. Figure 8-10 shows the 3ds Max I3D Exporter dialog.

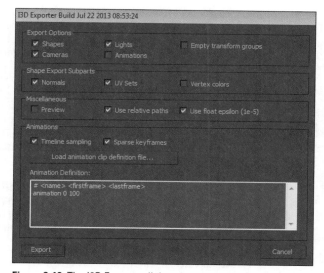

Figure 8-10: The I3D Exporter dialog gives you some options on how your scene is exported.

When you're satisfied with the settings in the exporter dialog, click the Export button to have an I3D file ready for opening in GIANTS Editor.

Exporting with FBX

New to GIANTS Editor 6.0 is another way to use 3D content out of Blender, Maya, 3ds Max, and even a few other DCC applications. GIANTS Editor supports the FBX file format, an interchange format owned by Autodesk.

FBX is available as an export option for nearly all modern 3D DCC tools. Granted, some programs support FBX more completely than others, but if you're using a program that doesn't have an I3D exporter, such as Modo, Cinema4d, or Softimage, FBX is the best option you have available. In some cases, like if you're using Maya LT, which is a light-weight version of Maya geared specifically toward pro-ducing video game assets, FBX is your *only* export option (GIANTS Editor doesn't yet support the OBJ format).

Consult the documentation of your 3D program to get specifics on how much of the FBX format is supported and the exact steps you take to export. That said, the following outlines the basic steps for exporting to FBX in Blender, Maya, and 3ds Max:

- ✔ **Blender**: Make sure you have the FBX exporter add-on enabled (it's enabled by default). Then choose File⇨Export⇨Autodesk FBX (.fbx) from the menu. Options for the FBX format are available on the left region of the File Browser.

- ✔ **Maya:** Choose File⇨Export All from the menu and set the Files of type drop-down menu to FBX export from the file browser dialog. Options for the FBX format are available on the right side of the file browser dialog.

- ✔ **3ds Max**: Click the Max button and choose Export⇨ Export. From the file browser dialog, set your output destination and pick Autodesk (*.FBX) from the Save as type drop-down menu. When you click Save, a new dialog window appears with options for export-ing to the FBX format.

Figure 8-11 shows the various FBX configuration options in each of these three programs.

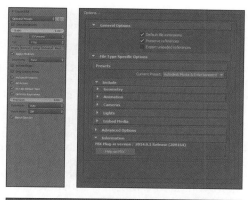

Figure 8-11: FBX export options for Blender, Maya, and Max.

Importing Your Mod into GIANTS Editor

You're now ready to get your files into a proper mod. If you exported an I3D file, you can immediately test the export by opening it directly in GIANTS Editor. You can either double-click the file in your operating system's file manager (Windows Explorer in Windows, Finder in Mac OS X) or you can open the file from within GIANTS Editor using the File menu (File⇨Open).

The more common scenario is that you've already started a mod and you're pulling more 3D content into it. For that, the preferred method is to use File⇨Import from the menu in GIANTS Editor. Doing so brings up a file browser dialog that allows you to choose either an I3D or FBX file to bring into your scene. Simply navigate to the file you want, select it, and click the Open button. Assuming the I3D or FBX file is properly formatted (if it's not properly formatted, you'll get an error and you'll need to try to reexport your model, probably with different options enabled), you should see your 3D object open and viewable in GIANTS Editor.

If you open or import an I3D file and you only see a black silhouette of your object, don't worry. Nothing is broken. You just need to add a light to your scene (Create⇨Light) to make the surface materials and textures of your 3D object visible within the editor.

Part III
Enhancing Your Mods

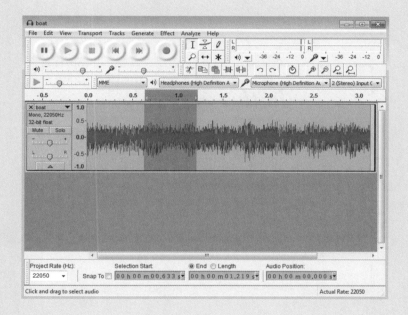

In this part . . .

✔ Understand why paying close attention to detail can set your mod apart from other mods

✔ Discover all of the various ways to add (and fake!) detail in your mod using textures

✔ Play with the new way that GIANTS Engine handles specular maps

✔ Bring that extra bit of polish to your mods by providing clean, accurate, and well-edited sounds

Chapter 9

Adding Texture to Your Mod

· ·

In This Chapter

▶ Using correctly sized images

▶ Adding textures to your 3D model

▶ Introducing ambient occlusion

▶ Utilizing textures efficiently

· ·

*T*extures are an important part of 3D computer graphics because they have the capability to bring life and variety to a world that's otherwise filled with flat colors on flatter surfaces. Textures tend to carry the weight of the game's realism in video game graphics. Graphics turn a simple cube into a beat-up wooden crate, a flat plane into the corona glow around a light, or a simple cylinder into a rolled-up bale of hay. Having high quality textures on your mod is pretty vital to getting it to look good and feel right in the Farming Simulator world.

This chapter gives you the information you need to have properly formatted textures so your mod can have increased realism without bogging down the game engine.

Working in Proper Texture Sizes

As a game engine, GIANTS Engine is capable of performing well even on computers with relatively modest hardware specifications. That's great news because more people can play and enjoy Farming Simulator — and by extension, your mod. As with anything, however, that benefit does come with a trade-off.

In this case, one of the trade-offs relates to the dimensions of image textures. Specifically, both the height and the width of your image, in pixels, must be a number that's a power of two. That is, the height and the width of your image must be one of the numbers as follows:

Power of 2 (2^n)	*Texture Size (in pixels)*
2^1	2
2^2	4
2^3	8
2^4	16
2^5	32
2^6	64
2^7	128
2^8	256
2^9	512
2^{10}	1,024
2^{11}	2,048

The largest-possible size for the height or width of a texture image in GIANTS Engine is 2,048 pixels. If both the height and width of the texture is 2,048 pixels, it's sometimes referred to as a *2k texture*.

Note, however, that the image doesn't have to be square. That is, although both the height and the width must be powers of two, they don't have to be the same value. As an example, just because the width of your text is 2,048 pixels, the height doesn't have to be. It can be 256 pixels, for example. Figure 9-1 shows a diagram of available image sizes and a valid texture within those dimensions.

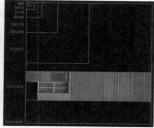

Figure 9-1: A grid of the available texture sizes in GIANTS Engine (left) and a properly sized texture (right).

Understanding the Texture Types Used on a Mod

GIANTS Engine uses three basic material properties: *diffuse* (color), *specular* (shininess), and *normal* (bumpiness). Refer to Chapter 4 for more details on material types. Although GIANTS Editor gives you the ability to set specific colors and values for these properties, you can use image textures to have a lot more control. This section is how to wield that control.

When naming your image textures, the convention is to start the filename with your mod's name and suffix it with the type of texture that it is. For example, if the model you're texturing is called `myFantasticMod`, then each of the three main texture files for it should have the names like so:

- ✔ myFantasticMod_diffuse.png
- ✔ myFantasticMod_specular.png
- ✔ myFantasticMod_normal.png

Know the difference between lossless and lossy compression

Wherever possible, do your image texture work in an image format with *lossless compression*, such as PNG (pronounced *ping*). Images with lossless compression use algorithms for shrinking the hard drive space consumed by an image without throwing away any data. Images using *lossy compression*, such as JPEG and DDS, save space by removing data that the algorithm thinks you won't notice.

Lossless compression image formats tend to be larger, but you're assured that your image won't suffer from *generation loss*, or degrading, each time you save because of recompressing. Image formats with lossy compression are best as final deliverables because they can take up substantially less memory and hard drive space. Short version: Work on your textures in PNG; release your mod with DDS textures. Refer to the "Optimizing Textures for the Game" section later in this chapter for more information.

And it's best to have all of your textures in a subfolder named `textures` within your main mod folder. This way all of your textures are in one place, and they're not cluttering up the space in the root of your mod folder.

Coloring with diffuse maps

If your object is going to have any texture image at all, it really should be a diffuse map. As mentioned in Chapter 7, even window materials support having a diffuse texture, rather than just adjusting color and transparency sliders.

This section provides you with the information necessary to prepare and create your own diffuse image textures.

Discussing digital color

It's important to have a solid comprehension of how digital images work if you want to use them effectively as textures. And to understand digital images, you need to know how computers handle color.

Most digital images — especially when it comes to video games — are RGB images, named for the three primary colors in light: red, green, and blue. The light primaries are used (instead of the pigment primaries of red, yellow, and blue that you may have learned in grade school) because computer monitors work by emitting light.

The light primaries in an image are *channels*. Using an image-editing program like Photoshop, you can see these channels. They're actually grayscale images, or *masks,* that represent how much influence that a primary color has on the overall image; lighter pixels represent a greater influence whereas darker pixels represent a lower influence. The following figure shows the corresponding red, green, and blue channels in a mod's store icon.

Red	Green	Blue

A fourth channel, the *alpha channel,* is also present in some images. A grayscale mask also represents this channel, just like the red, green, and blue channels. In this case, though, the mask doesn't represent the influence of a color, it represents the overall opacity of the image. White pixels are completely opaque whereas black pixels are fully transparent. Gray pixels fall in the spectrum between the two. Images with an alpha channel are sometimes referred to as *RGBA images*.

(continued)

(continued)

So for example, open up the sample mod that comes in the `sdk` folder where Farming Simulator is installed on your computer. Look into the textures folder at `window_diffuse.dds`. (Photoshop should open up this file without issue, but otherwise there are free DDS viewers available for download online. A developer from Nvidia has a nice one called WTV.) Looking at that image texture, you should notice that it's small at 16x16 pixels; its RGB channels set it to being a somewhat light blue. The alpha channel on this image is ever so slightly lighter than full black. That means the window is a mostly transparent light blue. For confirmation, you can load the mod in GIANTS Editor and have a look at the Materials panel with the windows selected.

Preparing to paint

To create diffuse maps on my 3D models, I like to lay down the groundwork in 3D and then paint my details in a 2D program like Photoshop, Paint.NET, or GIMP. Some people prefer to do the whole painting process in 3D and the available tools for doing so have matured quite a bit. In fact, depending on the 3D format, even Photoshop will allow you to paint directly on 3D objects. However, I actually still like doing it the old-school way.

If you have the ability to paint in 3D and prefer to work that way, refer to your software documentation for details. This section describes the more traditional process. As you become more advanced, you can easily switch between techniques to fit the situation. This chapter uses Blender as the primary 3D tool, but the same basic process works in other major software as well.

Chapter 7 explains how to set up your 3D scene and unwrap your model. Hide all objects other than the one you want to paint. The quick way to do that would be to select your desired object and press Numpad-slash (/) to enter Local View. Chances are good that when you do so, you also end up hiding your lamp, so your model goes back to being a black blob when looking at it with Textured Viewport Shading (Alt+Z).

Not to worry, you don't need the light for this step. Instead, select your object, go to the Shading panel in Material Properties, and enable the Shadeless checkbox. Doing so kills any highlights and shadows on your model, but it also ensures that your texture is completely visible.

Your object doesn't have texture yet, so you need to add an image texture to your object's material or you're not going to be painting on much of anything. Use the following steps to add a new diffuse texture to your model:

1. **Select your object.**

2. **From Texture Properties, select the first texture slot and click the New button below the list box.**

   When doing this step, make sure you see material textures and not world or brush textures. After clicking New, the rest of Texture Properties fills in with a bunch of additional panels.

3. **Name your texture using GIANTS convention (for example, `myFantasticMod_diffuse`).**

   Get in the habit of naming things and stay in the habit.

4. **Change the texture type to Image or Movie.**

   New textures default to being Clouds. You want an image.

5. **In the Image panel, click the New button.**

   This step pops up a little minidialog that asks for some details about your image. Fill it in as follows:

   • **Name:** Use the same name as your texture (for example, `myFantasticMod_diffuse`).

   • **Width/Height:** You need to pick these values now. There are a few optimal ways to do it, but for now just set it to the largest size GIANTS Engine can use (2,048x2,048 pixels). You can always resize the image later.

   • **Color:** This value sets the base color for the texture. I tend to leave the color at the default black.

- **Alpha:** If your texture requires transparency (like a window), enable this checkbox. Otherwise, you can disable it.

- **Generated Type:** The default here is Blank, which works fine, but I prefer to use the Color Grid type. It gives me a visual reference so I know where on my 2D texture I'm painting. It's all getting painted over anyway, so prepopulating your pixels with something useful doesn't hurt.

- **32-bit Float:** This option is for textures that require a lot of color precision. Because those textures aren't typically used in games, go ahead and leave this checkbox disabled.

6. **In the Mapping panel, change the Coordinates drop-down menu from Generated to UV.**

   This step ensures that your new texture uses the UV coordinates from your unwrap process. Assuming that all went well and you're using Textured Viewport Shading in the 3D View, you should have something that looks similar to Figure 9-2.

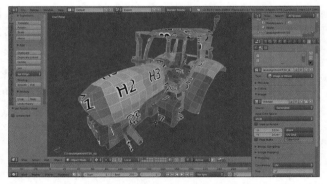

Figure 9-2: A new diffuse image texture added to an object in Blender.

With your texture unwrapped, it's a good idea to switch to a screen layout that better facilitates painting. I like to work from the UV Editing screen layout (from the Default layout, press Ctrl+Right Arrow four times or just use the Screens drop-down menu at the top of the Blender window). You have the texture assigned to your object's material, but you also need to make the association in a way that Blender's texture painting system understands.

Basically, you need to set the image in the UV/Image Editor while your object is in Edit mode. Use these steps:

1. **Select your object.**

2. **Toggle into Edit mode (Tab).**

3. **In the UV/Image Editor, use the image datablock drop-down menu to choose the new image you created.**

4. **Tab back into Object mode.**

You're ready to paint, but before doing so, I strongly recommend that you save this image to an external PNG file before starting (Image⇨Save as Image from the UV/Image Editor's header menu). As it currently stands, Blender still thinks that this image is automatically generated, not something that you intend on manually editing. By saving it to an external file, Blender understands that the image is editable. And more importantly, you remember that you need to regularly save this image as you work.

Painting diffuse maps

You are finally ready to start painting. In the 3D View, change from Object mode to Texture Paint mode using the Mode drop-down menu in its header at the bottom of the window. You should see brush settings appear in the Tool Shelf along the left side of the 3D View and an overlay of your UV layout in the UV/Image Editor. Also, while in the UV/Image Editor, you may want to hide its Properties region (N), show its Tool Shelf (T), and switch its interaction mode from View to Paint using the drop-down menu at the bottom of the window. Your screen should look something like Figure 9-3.

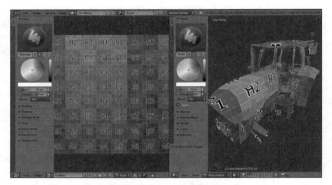

Figure 9-3: A Blender layout ready for painting.

Your brush settings are synced between the 3D View and the UV/Image Editor, so you can quickly switch back and forth, painting in whichever editor is most appropriate. And as you do so, the other editor updates simultaneously so you can see the results of your painting.

Some artists choose to paint their entire model this way, which is especially nice if you have a graphics tablet with a pen. Using this type of tablet makes it feel a lot more like a painting and drawing experience. Combined with Blender's masking and painting tools, you can add quite a bit of detail. For myself, I prefer to use this painting technique as a means of painting in a base coat, blocking in the rough colors and placement that I want on the model. I paint broad colors in the 3D View and clean edges and seams in the UV/Image Editor (saving both the PNG image and the .blend file as I go). Then, after you're satisfied with the base color scheme, you can save that external PNG file and open it in a more traditional 2D image editor, such as Photoshop, Paint.NET, or GIMP, and continue to add details.

When you work on your texture in a 2D image editor, you may miss having the overlay of your UV layout. Knowing what part of your object you're painting can be handy. Fortunately, Blender can help you get your overlay back. If you toggle into Edit mode (Tab) and change the UV/Image Editor's interaction mode from Paint back to View, you can choose UVs⇨Export UV Layout from the header menu (you may need to enable the Export UV Layout add-on from User Preferences to see this menu option). Now you can load your object's UV layout as a separate layer in Photoshop and use it as a frame of reference.

As you update your texture in your 2D image editor, periodically save or export your work back to the PNG image. If you do, you can choose Image⇨Reload Image from the UV/Image Editor's header menu (or press Alt+R) in Blender, and the texture will update in on your model so you can see the results of your hard work.

When you finish texture painting, make sure you disable the Shadeless checkbox on your object's material so it reacts properly to light and shadows again. You should also press Numpad-slash (/) to get out of Local View.

Adding details with normal maps

Adding a normal map texture to your object doesn't require a PhD. All you need is a generated normal map. (Chapter 7 explains what normal maps are and how you can generate one.) Applying a normal map to your model does have a couple of nuances compared to adding a diffuse map. Here are the steps you need to follow:

1. **Select your object.**

2. **In Texture Properties, select an unused texture slot and add a new texture.**

3. **Name your new texture according to GIANTS convention (for instance, `myFantasticMod_normal`).**

4. **Change the image type to Image or Movie.**

5. In the Image panel, click Open and use the File Browser to find your normal map image.

6. In the Mapping panel, change Coordinates from Generated to UV.

7. In the Influence panel, disable the Diffuse Color checkbox and enable the checkbox next to Normal in the Geometry section.

8. Sit back and revel in your awesomeness.

Adjusting shininess with specular maps

A specular map is a deceptively simple texture to paint. A *specular map* is a grayscale image that controls the *specularity,* or shininess, of your material. Values closer to white have more specularity, whereas values closer to black have less; they're more matte.

Think about the materials that make up your model. In general, metal and automotive paint have higher specularity, whereas rubber nonslip surfaces and old, worn wood have low specularity. However, nothing is quite that simple. Metals and paints get dull as they age. In contrast, some rough surfaces can start gaining some shine as they get smoothed out from use. You have to think not only about the types of materials in your object, but also the age you intend for them to appear to have.

After you figure out the details about your object's material, you can paint the specular map using the same basic process you use for painting diffuse maps, with a few subtle differences. Here's the breakdown on the steps to set it up:

1. Select your object.

2. In Texture Properties, select a texture slot that isn't already in use and add a new texture.

3. Name your new texture something sensible (for example, `myFantasticMod_specular`).

4. Change the texture type to Image or Movie.

5. Create a new image in the Image panel.

   Leave the Generated Type as Blank.

6. In the Mapping panel, change the coordinates drop-down menu from Generated to UV.

7. In the Influence panel, disable the checkbox next to Diffuse Color and enable the checkbox for Specular Color.

With your texture properly set up, you can paint your specular map using the same process as painting the diffuse map (refer to the earlier section, "Painting diffuse maps"). The only difference in this case: You're starting with a blank, black image instead of the color grid. And when you paint, you only add levels of gray and white, effectively telling the render engine to make those parts of the mesh shinier.

When you finish, save your specular map to an image file using the GIANTS convention (for instance, `myFantastic mod_specular.png`). Figure 9-4 shows an example of what a finished specular map might look like.

What you just produced is the simplest form of a specular map. It works fine in the basic case, but you can create a supercharged specular map specifically for GIANTS Engine. Not only does it include specularity, but it also provides texture information for ambient occlusion and dirt. The next two sections cover the process of creating these other texture types and the section "Assembling a Complete Specular Map" covers how to pull them all together into a single image that GIANTS Engine can understand.

Figure 9-4: A completed basic specular map for a tractor.

Baking ambient occlusion textures

Inspect the world around you, and pay attention to how light bounces all around, reflecting off of everything and subtly brightening everything. Minor bits of reflected light let you see details you may not otherwise notice. In computer graphics, this phenomenon is referred to as *global illumination*. The general case involves subtle increases in ambient light, but global illumination also covers more interesting cases like light bouncing off a green wall and thereby giving the rest of the room a slightly greenish hue.

Generating global illumination effects can be an incredibly computer-intensive process, and most video game engines don't support any kind of full-blown global illumination. That said, global illumination has another side effect that many game engines *can* take advantage of. Go back to inspect-the-world mode. Perhaps you're reading this text in an actual book (as opposed to an e-reader). If you are, keep the book open and arbitrarily rotate the book around in front of you. Notice that no matter how much light is bouncing around and adding extra light to everything, the seam at the center of the book consistently remains darker than the pages. Looking up from the book, you should be able to see this in other places, too: shelves close to walls, cracks in the sidewalk, even interior corners of rooms.

What you're observing is a side effect of global illumination. In computer graphics, this effect is often referred to as *ambient occlusion (AO)*. Ambient occlusion is most certainly not global illumination. However, the effect can be created pretty quickly and, more importantly, that effect can be baked into a texture, kind of like a normal map.

Generally speaking an AO map is a grayscale image wherein dark pixels are surface details that tend to remain dark and light pixels are surface areas that are typically smoother and remain light. Traditionally, most game engines don't use AO maps directly. You've had to mix them with your diffuse map, directly influencing your model's color. In GIANTS Engine, however, AO maps *are* used directly. They just happen to be packed into the specular map.

You first need to generate your AO map. You can typically do it by using the rendering engine built into your 3D modeling program. This way you can add surface details to your diffuse map without painting them by hand. It's even truer if you're already using a high-resolution model to generate a normal map.

The steps you take to generate, or *bake,* an AO map are roughly the same as the ones you use to bake a normal map:

1. **Select the object for which you want to bake an AO map.**

2. **Toggle into Edit mode (Tab).**

3. From the UV/Image Editor, create a new blank image at your desired size.

4. Toggle back into Object mode (Tab).

5. In World Properties, make sure Ambient Occlusion is enabled.

6. (Optional) In the Ambient Occlusion panel, change the Blend Mode drop-down menu from Add to Multiply.

7. (Optional) In World Properties, enable Environment Lighting and set the Energy value to 0.5.

   Technically, it's more accurate to leave the Blender Mode and Environment Lightning properties at their default values, but I find that these settings generate more pleasant results.

8. In the Gather panel of World Properties, change the Sampling drop-down menu from Constant QMC to Adaptive QMC (this step typically yields cleaner results).

9. Still in the Gather panel, enable Falloff and adjust the Strength value to taste.

   I like to start at 5.0 and tweak from there.

10. In Render Properties, go to the Bake panel and change the Bake Mode to Ambient Occlusion.

11. Still in the Bake panel, click the Bake button and wait for your AO map to finish being generated (depending on the detail of your mesh, it may take a while).

Figure 9-5 shows an AO bake for a tractor. For kicks, I've also applied the AO map as a shadeless texture on the model so you can see what it looks like when applied.

Figure 9-5: Ambient occlusion baked to a texture for a tractor model.

If you have collision meshes for your mod, disable their visibility both in the 3D View and when rendering. If you don't, the proximity of those collision meshes will make your AO bake look quite wonky. You may also want to separate possible moving parts into their own objects to prevent static shadows in your bake.

Save your texture to a real PNG image outside of Blender. Not only is it how you can guarantee that your bake is saved, but it also is what you need to merge the AO bake with your specular map in Photoshop. And although GIANTS Editor doesn't directly use this texture, that's no reason to break convention. Name your AO texture something like `myFantasticMod_ao.png`.

Using the dirt channel

The dirt map is a new feature supported by GIANTS Engine. A *dirt map* is basically a grayscale image that indicates how dirt can appear on various parts of your model. Like the AO map, the dirt map is ultimately combined with the specular map. First, however, you need to paint it.

To paint a dirt map, you use the exact same steps you use to create the specular map. The only difference is in how you paint. Rather than painting gray values to control how shiny each part of your object is, a dirt map uses those gray values to control dirt placement. Darker pixels are cleaner, whereas lighter pixels represent having more dirt. While you paint, you may also want to consider how that dirt gets there. The dirt could appear over time from wear and age, or a tractor wheel could have kicked up dirt. Figure 9-6 shows a completed dirt map.

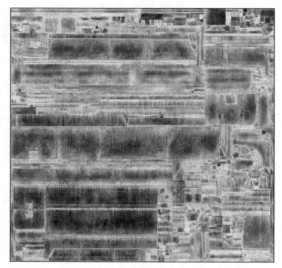

Figure 9-6: Dirt maps show where and how your 3D model gets dirty.

When you finish painting your dirt map, save it to a PNG image using the GIANTS convention, so something like `myFantasticMod_dirt.png`.

Assembling a Complete Specular Map

You've painted or baked textures for your specular, ambient occlusion, and dirt maps. These textures are saved in separate images, with names something like the following:

> ✔ myFantasticMod_specular.png
>
> ✔ myFantasticMod_ao.png
>
> ✔ myFantasticMod_dirt.png

Unfortunately, GIANTS Engine can't use these images directly. You must combine them into a single image, specifically the specular map image. To do it, you have to use a neat trick that takes advantage of the fact that all three images are grayscale. In fact, stop thinking of them as images. Instead, think of them as grayscale representations of information. The specular map is a grayscale representation of shininess, the AO map represents ambient lighting effects, and the dirt map, most obviously, represents dirt buildup.

Most digital images consist of three color channels: red, green, and blue. You can think of each of those channels as grayscale representations of how much each of those colors influence the overall image. What if you didn't use those channels to represent colors? What if you used them to represent information like shininess, light, and dirt? If so, you would have a way to combine three maps into a single image.

The image itself may look quite strange, but this use of the red, green, and blue channels is exactly what GIANTS Engine expects you to do for the specular map image.

You need to edit your specular image, mapping data to each color channel as the following table shows:

Color Channel	Texture Map
Red	Roughness (specular)
Green	Ambient occlusion
Blue	Dirt

The process you use to assign each texture to its own channel is pretty straightforward in Photoshop. Use the following steps:

1. **Open your specular image (for example, myFantasticMod_specular.png) in Photoshop.**

2. **In the Channels window, select the Green and Blue channels.**

   The overall image should turn a slightly green-blue color, and the Red channel should appear to be disabled.

3. **On your image, select all (Ctrl+A).**

4. **Fill this selection with black (Edit⇨Fill).**

   You should notice that the Green and Blue channels are black whereas your specular texture is still on the Red channel.

5. **Open your ambient occlusion image (for example, myFantasticMod_ao.png).**

6. **Select all in your AO image (Ctrl+A) and copy it to the clipboard (Ctrl+C).**

7. **Switch back to your specular image and select only the Green channel in the Channels window.**

8. **Paste your AO texture (Ctrl+V).**

   You should now be able to cycle through the channels and notice that your specular data is on Red, AO data is on Green, and the Blue channel is still blank.

9. Use the same process in Steps 5–8, but for your *dirt map,* and paste that data into the *Blue* channel.

10. Save your specular image (for example, `myFantasticMod_specular.png`) and you're good to go.

When GIANTS Editor loads your specular image, it automatically knows how to handle each of the channels, so there's no additional work for you to do there. Pretty clever stuff, huh?

Optimizing Textures for the Game

Because you're creating these 3D assets and textures for a video game mod, you should make sure you're making the most efficient use of memory, hard drive space, and computer processing power. Specific to GIANTS Engine and Farming Simulator, two optimizations for textures go the furthest in terms of maintaining good gameplay performance:

- ✔ **Choose the right-sized texture for the job.** This optimization doesn't just pertain to obvious things, like avoiding the use of a 2,048x2,048 pixel texture on a stone that, in-game, is never larger than half a meter. But some texture types also don't require as much detail. For instance, specular maps can often be large flat colors. You may be able to get away with an image that's half the size of your diffuse texture for the same object.

- ✔ **Use DirectDraw Surface (DDS) as the *deliverable* file format when you release your mod.** Although the DDS format uses a lossy compression algorithm that isn't ideal for regular editing, it *is* optimized for computer video hardware, and DDS files are typically much smaller than PNGs. The rest of this section is devoted to this form of optimization.

Although programs like Blender, Maya, and 3ds Max have
no problem working with DDS files, your typical 2D image
editor doesn't have native support for them. In fact, for
Photoshop, you need to download a specialized plugin that
allows Photoshop to read and write DDS files. Fortunately,
it's free. You can get this plugin from the Nvidia website.
Go to `https://developer.nvidia.com` and click on
the link for Nvidia Gameworks. When that page loads,
look for a menu labeled Tools. Click on it and choose the
Texture Tools for Adobe Photoshop link (alternatively,
you can type in the direct URL: `https://developer.`
`nvidia.com/nvidia-texture-tools-adobe-`
`photoshop`).

Download and install the plugin on your computer. It
should work just fine with the latest Photoshop CC and
as far back as Photoshop 5.0. After you have the plugin
installed, you can use Photoshop to convert all of your
project PNG textures to DDS format prior to releasing
your mod. This also gets rid of a few annoying warnings
when you load your mod in GIANTS Editor.

After you convert your textures to DDS, you *don't* need
to make sure your mod points to the DDS files instead of
the PNGs. Both GIANTS Engine and GIANTS Editor automatically look in the same folder as your PNG and to see
whether a corresponding DDS file exists as well.

Chapter 10

Working with Sounds

●●

In This Chapter

▶ Obtaining sounds for your mod

▶ Preparing audio files for GIANTS Engine

▶ Putting sounds in your mod

●●

*G*reat video games are more than just a visual medium. They try to incorporate as many senses as possible, with hearing being one of the most important. Ambient noise gives a game environment life. Event-triggered sounds give players feedback, letting them know that they've done something in the game. Vehicle and character sounds can help players figure out where those things are in the game.

So to make your mod feel authentic, polished, and complete, you need to include sounds. For example, if you have a vehicle or machine, you should have sound for that piece of equipment, or if you have a field on a custom map, perhaps you can make crickets chirp when the player is near. Sound is important, and this chapter explains how you can obtain sounds and then incorporate them into your mod.

Getting Your Sounds

When obtaining sounds, you need to have sounds that appropriately match your mod, which is even truer with a modern game such as Farming Simulator. Modern gamers expect a certain level of realism in 3D games. As a modder, you should deliver on that expectation of quality.

But where do you find sounds for your mods? Realistically, you have two options: get them yourself or get them from someone else. The following sections explain in greater depth.

Recording your own sounds

By far, the best way to get the sounds you want is to record them yourself. When GIANTS Software made Farming Simulator 2015, it had people go out to manufacturers of farming equipment and record the exact sounds of the various machinery included in the game. In the process they even burned up one of their microphones with the exhaust heat from one of the tractors. Figure 10-1 shows a photo from one of these recording sessions.

Figure 10-1: Recording the sound of a tractor on-site.

Fortunately you don't need to run out and buy a collection of microphones and cabling. As an independent modder, you can make do with what you have. Even a mic on your mobile phone is a starting point. As you get more serious about modding, you can look into possibly renting audio equipment or purchasing a portable field recorder. Prices on these devices are reasonable, with entry-level ones starting at less than $100. If you want to purchase one, search online for "field recorder" to see your options.

What actually may be more difficult is getting access to the machinery that you want to record. Not everyone lives near a farm or knows a person who works for a farm equipment manufacturer. That said, people are generally friendly and reasonable if you approach them in a polite, professional manner and clearly explain what you want to do.

Assuming you have some basic recording gear and you've acquired permission to record, these tips can help ensure your recordings are high quality:

- **Isolate the sound you want from all other sounds.** Despite how they make it look in film and TV shows, separating sounds in a single audio track without degrading the overall quality of the recording isn't easy. So you want to try do your recording away from all other sounds. If you have a directional mic, like a shotgun mic, be sure to aim it directly at the source of your sound.

- **Use headphones while recording.** Most recording gear has a jack for connecting headphones. Use it. And use the best quality headphones you can get your hands on, preferably ones that fully cover your ears and isolate them from outside noise. Having a great microphone does you no good if you have no idea what sounds it's actually recording.

- **Record more than you need.** Record the sound multiple times and record it for a longer duration than you need. You can always edit a sound to be shorter; getting multiple takes of a sound ensures you're not stuck with a version of the sound that has a train running in the background, for example.

✔ **Record room tone.** *Room tone* is a term for the sound of silence at the location where you've also recorded the sounds you actually want. That is, you should turn off all machinery at the site and record 30 to 60 seconds. Room tone is valuable when editing sound. Aside from being in a vacuum, no place is soundless, and microphones often pick up on things that you may not notice until you're trying to splice two sounds together, and you then notice an awkward jump in background noise.

Searching online

If you don't have any recording gear or you don't want to hassle with recording your own sounds, you can go online for sounds. You can pay a number of companies for sounds, but you may even be able to get your sounds for free.

Consider starting at these two websites:

✔ `www.freesound.org`: This site is one of the best places to go for sounds. It hosts a searchable database of all manner of sounds. And most importantly, they're all available under a Creative Commons (CC) license. What that means for you is that all the sounds on the site are free to download and use in your mods.

✔ `www.creativecommons.org`: If you want to find out more about the various CC licenses that may be in use, go to this site. It has clearly written explanations for what each license allows users to do. While at this site, you can also take advantage of the CC search feature `http://search.creativecommons.org`. This tool allows you to search multiple media websites for CC-licensed media, including sounds. A lot of the sound sites for CC content focus primarily on music, but you may come across the exact sound you're looking for with this search tool.

Editing Sound Files

Regardless of any sound editing you want to do and where you obtained your sounds, you have to do two things in order to prepare sounds for your mod:

- **Trim your audio.** As I suggest in the earlier section, "Recording your own sounds," you record more sound than you need. Now you must cut away the superfluous parts and, if necessary, make the sound loopable as well.

- **Mix down your audio to mono.** GIANTS Engine supports 3D stereo sound. However, the engine determines which speaker plays the sound, not the sound file. In fact, if the engine detects a stereo sound file, it automatically converts it to mono anyway. So it does you no good to have a file with stereo sound; it just wastes hard drive space.

You can do both in nearly any audio-editing program. A popular choice is the free and open source sound editor, Audacity. You can download an installer for it from the Audacity website (`http://audacity.sourceforge.net`).

After you install Audacity, start it and open one of your sound files (File➪Open). The first time you open a sound file in Audacity, you'll get a warning dialog that gives you the choice between making a copy of your file before editing and reading your file directly. Audacity recommends the former as being a safer way to work. Use your own discretion and click OK after you make your choice. Figure 10-2 shows this warning dialog.

Figure 10-2: Audacity suggests that you work from a copy of your sound file rather than the original.

The Audacity interface isn't overly complex. If you click and drag over your sound's waveform, you can highlight parts of it, which is the main process you use for trimming away the extraneous parts of your sound file. Simply highlight the segment you wish to remove and then press Delete on your keyboard to remove it. Figure 10-3 shows the Audacity interface with part of a sound waveform highlighted and ready for removal.

When you remove a segment from the middle of a sound file, Audacity automatically shifts the remainder of the sound file left to fill the void. This is sometimes referred to as a *ripple edit* because your delete operation has an effect that ripples across the rest of the file.

The other edit you may need to do is the conversion to mono, which is super easy. Just go to Tracks➪Stereo Track to Mono in the menu. Audacity quickly handles the rest of the conversion for you.

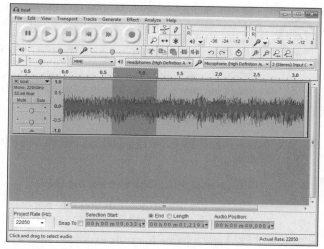

Figure 10-3: A sound file being edited in Audacity.

Exporting Sounds for GIANTS Engine

To export your sound, you need to get it out of Audacity and into a format that GIANTS Engine understands. Check the *sample rate* of your sound file. This number represents how frequently the digital sound matches the original, analog sound. With mono sounds, you can often get away with a value as low as 22.05 kHz. However CD-quality sound is 44.1 kHz. Either of these is supported by GIANTS Engine.

If you recorded your own sound, more than likely you recorded at either 44.1 kHz or 48 kHz. If you downloaded the sound from the Internet, the sample rate could be anything. Fortunately, Audacity tells you on the left of your waveform's track in the interface what the sample rate is. In Figure 10-3, the audio's sample rate is set at 22050Hz, or 22.05 kHz.

You can change a track's sample rate by going to Tracks⊏ Resample and entering your desired sample rate in the window that pops up. Be careful, though. If you dial down the sample rate too much, it can degrade the audio quality. And increasing a track's sample rate does nothing to improve the quality; it only wastes drive space. For export purposes, you also want to make sure the Project Rate at the bottom left of the Audacity window is also set to the same sample rate you want on output.

As for actually exporting your sound, just use these steps:

1. **Choose File⊏Export from the menu.**

2. **Use the file browser dialog that appears to navigate to your mod's folder on your hard drive.**

3. **Type a name for your exported sound file.**

4. **From the Save as type drop-down menu at the bottom of the dialog, choose WAV (Microsoft) signed 16-bit PCM.**

5. **Click the Save button and you're done.**

Bringing Sounds into Your Mod

To bring a properly trimmed and formatted sound file into GIANTS Editor and, ultimately, your mod, follow these steps:

1. **From GIANTS Editor, choose Create⊏AudioSource.**

2. **Navigate to the location on your hard drive where your sound file is and select it.**

   Really, this should be the same folder where the rest of your mod lives.

3. **Click Open.**

After you do these steps, an audio source is added to your scene. In the 3D Viewport, it looks like a little wireframe speaker in the center of a giant wireframe sphere. You should also be able to see it at the bottom of your Scenegraph, named *audio*. You can, of course, rename it from the Attributes panel and nest it within another object's hierarchy or transform group by using cut and paste in the Scenegraph. You also have a few audio-specific controls in the Audio tab of the Attributes panel, as shown in Figure 10-4.

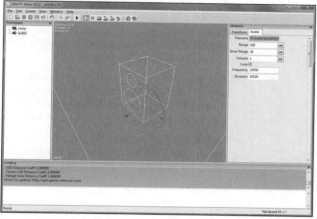

Figure 10-4: A newly created audio source in GIANTS Editor.

The following is a quick rundown of the settings available in the Audio tab of the Attributes panel:

- ✓ **Filename:** The path to your audio file. It isn't editable from within GIANTS Editor. The only way to change the path is to open the I3D file in a text editor like Notepad++. Deleting the audio source and readding it from its new location is often easier.

- ✓ **Range:** The radius, in meters, from the center of the audio source object so a player while in-game can hear the sound.

✓ **Inner range:** Sounds don't just turn off when you're out of range. They fade out. The inner range defines how far away from the audio source the fading begins. Realistically, sounds start fading immediately, but this is one of those cases where realism doesn't always give the best gameplay results.

✓ **Volume:** This number is multiplied by the internal *gain* or volume of the sound file. If your exported sound is too soft or too loud, you can adjust this value a bit. If you always change this setting, then you should make the edit in your original sound file so this parameter can stay at 1.

✓ **Loop:** Works as advertised. If this checkbox is enabled, the sound always *loops* or plays again from the start when it gets to the end.

✓ **Frequency:** This should be the sample rate of your sound file. This value is for informational purposes. It can't be edited from GIANTS Editor. Resampling needs to be done with your audio editing software.

✓ **Duration:** The length of your audio file, in milliseconds. Like Frequency, it's not editable and is only in the interface for informational purposes.

Part IV
Customizing Mod Behaviors

In this part . . .

✔ Define your own vehicles with a firm understanding of the structure in a custom vehicle XML file

✔ Understand how you can either add small new features or completely overhaul Farming Simulator using Lua

✔ Prepare your mods for actually being used in the in-game store by creating icons

✔ Share your mod with other modders and players in the Farming Simulator community

Chapter 11

Tweaking Vehicle XML

A large bulk of this book focuses its attention on the aesthetic components of your mod, but what about functionality? Sure, you have a sweet-looking custom tractor or trailer, but if it doesn't *do* anything that's different from the in-game vehicles, then you're only addressing half the fun of modding. Modding is about making customizations to the game — in essence, making it your own. In this case, it means taking a peek under the hood of your digital tractor and seeing how it works. Then you can start adjusting values and making improvements.

Under the hood you find the eXtensible Mark-up Language (XML). Chapter 6 explains how XML works and how big of a role it plays with GIANTS Engine. You should also have a decent text-editing program like Notepad++ installed on your computer.

In addition to `modDesc.xml`, each vehicle mod has a single XML file that describes its functionality. That XML file has the exact same name as your vehicle's I3D file, just with an `.xml` extension instead of `.i3d`.

The best way to familiarize yourself with vehicle XML files is to look at a few. Many examples are already on your hard drive. Not only is there the sample mod that comes in the `sdk` folder where Farming Simulator is installed (typically something like `C:\Program Files\Farming Simulator 2015`), but all of the vehicles that come with Farming Simulator also have XML files that you can inspect. They live in `data\vehicles` where you have Farming Simulator installed.

And if that's not enough, you can also have a look at the vehicle XML files for any Farming Simulator mod that you've downloaded. That said, most of this chapter uses the sample mod's vehicle XML file as the go-to reference.

Dealing with .xml filenames

On Windows computers in their default configuration, telling which file is an I3D file and which is an XML file is pretty difficult, especially if the files have the same base name. The only noticeable difference is the file's icon because Windows tries to be helpful and friendly by hiding the file name *extensions* (the last few letters in the filename after a period, for example in `modDesc.xml`, the `.xml` is the extension).

In my experience, this helpful hiding feature of Windows causes more confusion than it actually helps. Fortunately, there's a fix. From Windows Explorer, click the Organize button in the upper left of the window and choose *Folder and search options*. In the Folder Options dialog that pops up, go to the View tab and look for a checkbox labeled "Hide extensions for known file types." Disable that checkbox, and you can then see file extensions in any Windows Explorer window or file browser dialog.

Understanding Object Indexing

If you open mods and maps in GIANTS Engine, you may notice that having multiple different objects all sharing the same name is perfectly acceptable. GIANTS Engine doesn't use naming as a means of referencing objects. Instead, it uses something called an object's index path. The *index path* is a sequence of numbers, separated by symbols, that represents where an object is located in the scene hierarchy.

For example, open any I3D file in GIANTS Editor. (I recommend a large scene with a lot of objects in it, like a map.) With the file loaded, select any object and look over in the Transform tab of the Attributes panel. Figure 11-1 shows what you may see.

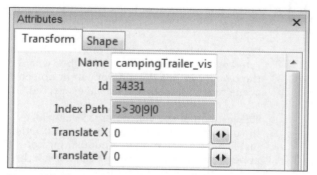

Figure 11-1: The Attributes panel in GIANTS Editor shows you your selection's index path.

The third field down is the index path, and it should have a value in it that looks similar to the one in Figure 11-2.

The first number followed by a greater-than symbol (>) in the index path is the *scene root,* or the parent object at the first level of the Scenegraph. If you collapse the whole tree in the Scenegraph, you can see all of the scene root objects. Clicking through them, you should see that they're numbered sequentially from top to bottom. The first object has a value of 0>, the second is 1>, and so on.

Scene Root   Parent Tree   Selected Object

Figure 11-2: Index paths follow a very specific numbering scheme.

Like most things involving computers and programming, counting for index paths starts at 0 rather than 1. So if an object has an index of 1, it's really the second object, not the first.

Figure 11-1 shows a series of more numbers, each separated with a pipe symbol (|), which is what I refer to as the *parent tree*. It's the path of parent objects from the scene root to the object you have selected.

The last number in that series is your selected object. If it's the only child, then that last number is 0. Otherwise, it's just like the scene root; that number indicates the order it appears in the Scenegraph (for instance, if the number is 3, then it's the fourth object). In a way, it's similar to drilling down the path in your file browser to find a specific file on your hard drive.

Because GIANTS Editor tells you the index path for your selection right in the interface, you can easily highlight this value and copy it for pasting in your vehicle XML file. Knowing what this number means is necessary for going in the reverse direction, up the scene hierarchy. When you come across an index path in the vehicle XML file, it may not be immediately obvious which object it is. But because you know how to decode the path, you can open the I3D file in GIANTS Editor and drill down through the Scenegraph to see which object it is.

To keep the index path straight, some modders like to prefix the object names with the last number in their index path. If you look at the sample mod that comes with Farming Simulator, you should see that objects are named with _00_, _01_, _02_, and so on at the front of each name. By doing it this way, you can look right in the Scenegraph and have an idea what the index path is for those subobjects.

Discovering the Structure of a Vehicle XML File

If you open the vehicle XML file that comes with the sample mod, you should notice that the top line is exactly like the first line in modDesc.xml:

```
<?xml version="1.0" encoding="utf-8"
          standalone="no" ?>
```

This code is standard XML and it's basically a notification that says, "Hi! I'm an XML file." Below the first line is the main tag for the whole file, <vehicle>. This tag has a single attribute, type. This attribute can be set to any of the default vehicle types that come with Farming Simulator, as the following list shows:

- attachableCombine
- baleLoader
- baler
- cart
- combine
- combine_cylindered
- cultivator
- cultivator_animated
- cutter
- cutter_animated
- defoliator_animated
- dynamicMount AttacherImplement
- dynamicMount AttacherTrailer
- forageWagon
- frontloader
- fuelTrailer
- implement
- implement_ animated

- manureBarrel
- manureSpreader
- milktruck
- mixerWagon
- mower
- mower_animated
- plough
- ridingMower
- selfPropelled MixerWagon
- selfPropelledMower
- selfPropelled PotatoHarvester
- selfPropelledSprayer
- shovel
- shovel_animated
- sowingMachine
- sowingMachine_ animated
- sprayer
- sprayer_animated
- sprayer_mouse Controlled
- strawBlower
- tedder
- telehandler
- tractor
- tractor_articulated Axis
- tractor_cylindered
- trafficVehicle
- trailer
- trailer_mouse Controlled
- waterTrailer
- wheelLoader
- windrower
- woodShredder

You can also set the `type` attribute to a custom vehicle type that you define in Lua.

All of the other sections are nested within the `<vehicle>` tag and are organized as follows:

- **Meta data:** These tags provide information about the vehicle. They include `<annotation>`, `<name>`, and `<filename>`. All of them are similar to the corresponding ones in `modDesc.xml`.

✔ **Wheels and motors:** These tags include the `<wheels>`, `<motor>`, `<fuelCapacity>`, and `<fuelUsage>` tags. They have the most control over how your vehicle moves.

✔ **Components:** If you have a complex vehicle mod, it may be composed of multiple objects or components. In this section, you can inform the physics system how to handle the objects' centers of mass and the quality of the physics calculations.

✔ **Cameras:** Players like to see from different views while driving vehicles. This section lets GIANTS Engine know where the cameras are and how much control the player has over them.

✔ **Lights:** This section controls how the lights on your vehicle affect the rest of the scene, or if they do at all. Included in this are the tags for `<lights>`, `<brakeLights>`, `<turnLights>`, `<reverseLights>`, and `<beaconLights>`.

✔ **Player-related:** These tags relate specifically to how the player interacts with the vehicle. Tags include `<steering>`, `<enterReferenceNode>`, `<exitPoint>`, `<size>`, and `<characterNode>`.

✔ **Attachments:** The `<attacherJoints>` tags dictate how and where a vehicle can have attachments.

✔ **Sounds:** Vehicles can incorporate a variety of sounds. Some of them don't require an audio source object, as I discuss in Chapter 10. This section is where you define those extra sounds such as sounds for the motor, horn, compressed air, and attaching.

Setting Correct Collisions

If you open the sample mod that comes with Farming Simulator, you should notice that a few objects render invisible. Some of them are *collision objects* for the vehicle mod, indicated by having `_col` as a suffix on their names. The wheels, the tractor's body, and the cab have a collision object, and a large box in front of the tractor is a collision object to detect vehicles ahead when driven by a helper.

Collision objects should be *convex,* meaning they shouldn't have parts of the mesh that cut in on themselves, like a cave. If you need that kind of shape, you can make a *compound object,* where you use multiple convex collision objects to define your shape.

GIANTS Engine uses these collision objects to trigger events and calculate physics. However, just having an unrenderable mesh in your Scenegraph isn't enough. The game engine needs to be made aware of that mesh's purpose as a collision object. Unfortunately, this process is a bit of mystical art involving bitmasks. In a way, it's similar to how you paint foliage, just with a lot more possible checkbox combinations. (Refer to Chapter 3 for more on painting foliage.) Basically, the *collision mask* is a bitmask that defines what your collision object can collide with.

To define an object as a collision object within GIANTS Editor, first select it and make sure the Rigid Body checkbox is enabled in the Transform table of the Attributes panel. With this checkbox enabled, a new tab, labeled Rigid Body, appears in the Attributes panel. Click on that tab and you should see something like what's in Figure 11-3.

The Collision Mask field is the first one after a set of checkboxes. Technically, you can manually type in a value, but you would *really* have to know what you're doing for that work. However, if you have a lot of the same kind of collision mask, you can copy and paste this value after you've set it for one of them. Make sure that the Collision checkbox is enabled and then click the ellipsis (. . .) to the right of the Collision mask field. Doing so yields a Collision Mask dialog like the one shown in Figure 11-4.

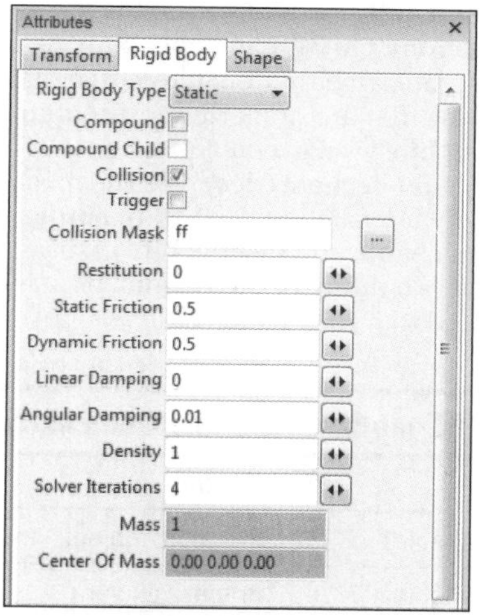

Figure 11-3: The Rigid Body tab of the Attributes panel is where you can define collision masks.

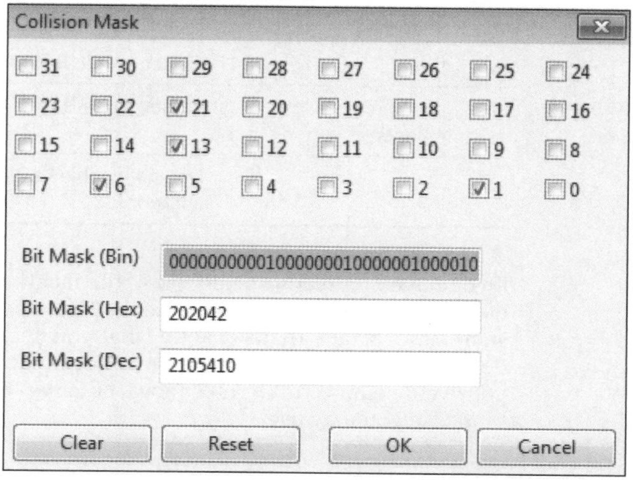

Figure 11-4: The Collision Mask dialog is where you do excellent bitmask-setting magic.

At the top of the Collision Mask dialog is a series of check-boxes labeled from 0 to 31. Each checkbox represents a single bit that you can either enable or disable. The three text fields below that are numeric representations of the combination of bits you've enabled in binary (bin), hexa-decimal (hex), and decimal (dec). For the most part, those fields are purely informational. They're automatically cal-culated as you enable and disable bits in mask. Table 11-1 gives a rough accounting of the various bitmask values and the features that they enable.

Table 11-1 Enabling Different Kinds of Collisions

Bit	Feature	Bit	Feature
1	non_pushable1	13	dynamic_objects_machines
2	non_pushable2	20	trigger_player
3	static_world1	21	trigger_tractors
4	static_world2	22	trigger_combines
6	tractors	23	trigger_fillables
7	combines	24	trigger_dynamic_objects
8	trailers	25	trigger_trafficVehicles
12	dynamic_ objects	26	trigger_cutters
		30	kinematic_objects_without_ collision

If you haven't already sorted it out, the fact that this mask of bits means that you can enable multiple ones at the same time. In fact, that's exactly what you need to do, depending on the type of collision objects you have in your vehicle mod. Table 11-2 shows common examples of bitmasks you may use.

Table 11-2	Example Bitmasks for Various Collision Types		
Collision Type	**Bits**	**Hex Value**	**Decimal Value**
Tractor	1, 6, 13, and 21	0x202042	2,105,410
Combine	1, 7, 13, and 22	0x402082	4,202,626
Fillable	1, 8, 13, and 23	0x802102	8,397,058
Cutter	1, 12, 13, 24, and 26	0x5003002	83,898,370
Tools	1, 13	0x2002	8194

The *0x* at the beginning of the hex value is there as standard notation to indicate that the number is hexidecimal rather than decimal or some other numbering scheme.

The bitmasks for the tractor, combine, and fillable in Table 11-2 assume you're setting them for the main body of those vehicles. If you're setting collision masks on subobjects like wheels, then the trigger bit in each of them isn't usually necessary. That is, for a tractor wheel collision mask, you only need to enable bits 1, 6, and 13. Bit 21 can remain disabled.

All of the exporters in Chapter 8 allow you to define the collision mask prior to exporting. However, for these exporters, you typically have to enter the hexidecimal value for the bitmask. The GIANTS Editor interface is currently the most straightforward means of setting the collision mask, so I suggest that you wait until after exporting to define your bitmask.

Working with Motors and Wheels

Your mod isn't much of a vehicle if it has no capability to go. It becomes a very attractive lawn ornament. The remedy to get your mod moving lies within the `<wheels>` and `<motor>` tags of your vehicle XML file, which these sections explain.

Focusing on the wheels

As a tag unto itself, the `<wheels>` tag only has a single attribute, `autoRotateBackSpeed`. This attribute defines the rate at which the steering wheel returns to the center when the player releases the steering controls.

Within the open and close of the `<wheels>` tag is a series of tags, appropriately called `<wheel>`, for each of the wheels in your vehicle. The following list goes through the main attributes for each `<wheel>` tag:

- ✔ **repr:** At the very least, every `<wheel>` tag must have this attribute. This is the index path to your vehicle's actual wheel object or its parent fender, but not the wheel's collision object.

- ✔ **driveNode:** If your wheel is a child of a fender, and that fender doesn't rotate, the `repr` attribute should be the fender's index path. This attribute should be the index path of your actual wheel object.

- ✔ **rotMax/rotMin:** These attributes dictate the limits of how much the wheels can rotate for steering purposes, which means that for nonsteering wheels, both of these attributes should be zero.

- ✔ **rotSpeed:** This rotation attribute dictates the maximum speed that a wheel can rotate when steering. If you have rear-wheel steering on your vehicle, set this attribute with a negative value.

- ✔ **radius:** You can measure your wheel's radius in your 3D modeling program (assuming you used real-world units) and enter that value, in meters, here.

- ✔ **suspTravel:** GIANTS Engine's physics system implements virtual springs (shock absorbers) on each wheel. This attribute controls the length of the spring that's suspending the wheel.

- ✔ **spring/damper:** These two attributes work together to control the physics properties of the virtual spring. Set the spring attribute too high and your vehicle bounces all over the place. Set the damper too high and your vehicle may cruise over even the roughest terrain like it's a paved road.

🗸 **deltaY:** The virtual spring is located at the center of the `repr` object and points downward along the *y*-axis, which causes your vehicle's wheels to push down. You can compensate for this effect using the `deltaY` attribute. As a starting point, set the value for this attribute to half the value used in the `suspTravel` attribute.

🗸 **maxLongStiffness/maxLatStiffness:** The stiffness attributes specifically relate to longitudinal and lateral friction of your vehicle's wheels. Friction is what allows wheels to move vehicles, so you should spend some time tweaking these attributes. Set them too high and your vehicle will be unable to move. Set them too low and it will feel like driving on ice.

🗸 **mass:** This value determines the rate the wheel can be accelerated by the motor. The higher the mass, the slower it will accelerate. A good starting value is 0.27.

Moving with your motor

The motor is the other half of the equation to making your vehicle move. Most of the motor's properties are contained within the `<motor>` tag's attributes and nested children tags. Two notable exceptions pertain to your vehicle's fuel. Incidentally, these two values are often one of the first things an early modder may try to change:

🗸 **<fuelCapacity>:** The number between the open and close of this tag is the maximum amount of fuel your vehicle can carry, in liters.

🗸 **<fuelUsage>:** Within the confines of this tag is a value that dictates how many liters of fuel your vehicle uses for each meter that it travels.

With the fuel parameters of your vehicle defined, the `<motor>` tag can draw your full attention. Unlike the `<wheels>` tag, most of your motor settings are attributes of the actual tag rather than child tags. The main reason is because vehicles only have one motor, so it makes sense. In the `<motor>` tag, the following are the main attributes with which you should concern yourself:

✓ **minRpm:** This attribute is the idle speed of your motor. Keep the value for this attribute relatively low. Otherwise, your vehicle will race off even when the player isn't stepping on the gas.

✓ **maxRpm:** The `maxRpm` attribute is a single value defining maximum rotations per minute (RPM) for the motor.

✓ **minForwardGearRatio/maxForwardGearRatio/ minBackwardGearRatio/maxBackwardGearRatio:** If you set the gear ratios to high values, you can make your vehicle's wheels spin faster when at a constant engine speed. The trade-off, however, is that higher gear ratios also require motors with more torque.

 If you go to the Farming Simulator Modding Tutorials that are available at the GIANTS Developer Network (`http:// gdn.giants-software.com/videoTutorials.php`), you can find a spreadsheet that helps you calculate correct RPM and gear ratio values for your motor. That spreadsheet can save you from wasting an immense amount of time tweaking those attributes by trial and error.

Setting Up Cameras

If your vehicle involves player interaction such as driving, the player is going to expect to be able to have at least one optimal viewing angle . . . and would prefer to have even more. To meet this expectation, you can set up cameras on your vehicle mod. However, just because you have camera objects in your I3D file, GIANTS Engine still doesn't quite know everything necessary to use them with your vehicle.

You need to inform the engine where the cameras are, as well as their capabilities. The `<cameras>` tag of your vehicle XML file handles it.

The way the cameras section of the XML file works, you use the count attribute in the `<cameras>` tag to inform the game engine of the number of cameras in your vehicle. Then, within the open and close of the `<cameras>` tag, you have a specific tag for each camera, numbered sequentially (for instance, `<camera1>`, `<camera2>`, and so on). The main attributes for each individual camera tag are as follows:

- ✔ **index:** Quite possibly the most important attribute, this index path goes to a camera object. Without it, GIANTS Engine doesn't know which camera you're talking about.

- ✔ **rotatable:** Typically this attribute is set as true. The only exception is something like a rear-view camera that's only used for backing up.

- ✔ **rotateNode:** Having your camera rotate about a set of axes other than its own, such as having an outdoor camera that points at your vehicle, is occasionally desirable. In that case, the camera should rotate about a point somewhere within the vehicle rather than its own local axes. In those situations, the `rotateNode` attribute is the index path of the alternate axes. For this to work properly, the camera object should be a child of whatever that `rotateNode` object is (typically a transform group).

The `rotateNode` attribute is useful when your camera is an outdoor camera, where it looks at the vehicle from outside of it rather than giving the player a first-person perspective from the driver's seat. However, when you set up an outdoor camera, GIANTS Engine has some automatic measures it takes to make using that camera more enjoyable for the player. Specifically, outdoor cameras purposefully avoid obstructions that may get between the camera and the vehicle. The engine moves the camera closer to the vehicle when it detects an obstruction getting in the way.

In order for this automated obstruction avoidance to work, though, the game engine needs one or more references. It needs to draw an imaginary line between the camera and some other object in the vehicle. This imaginary line is sometimes referred to as a *ray* that is *cast* from the camera to some reference point. The game engine makes sure that at least one reference point is visible to the camera. During gameplay, if another object crosses that ray, the game engine identifies an obstruction and moves the camera toward the vehicle.

To facilitate all of this in the vehicle XML file, you need to define a couple reference points, or *raycast nodes* (but not too many, casting too many rays can be computationally expensive) using a <raycastNode> tag as a child of your outdoor camera's tag. The <raycastNode> tag only has a single attribute, index, which is the index path of the object that the camera should cast a ray toward. Generally speaking, raycast node objects are transform groups, and you typically have one at the front of your vehicle and one at the rear.

Adding Lights

In addition to cameras, player-driven vehicles usually also have lights. They have to be able to see when they're working their fields in those dim hours before dawn, right? The <lights> section in your vehicle's XML file is where those lights are defined and controlled.

The <lights> tag itself has no attributes, but nested within it are child <light> tags, each one defining a single light in your vehicle. Each <light> tag has up to four attributes:

✔ **realLight:** This attribute is the index path to an actual light object in the I3D file. Real lights take more processing power, so you don't want to have too many on your vehicle. In-game, only two are ever used at the same time.

✔ `fakeLight`: A fake light offers no real illumination to the scene, so it takes much less processing power. Typically fake lights are boxes or cones with a gradient texture that looks like light emanating from a source. The `fakeLight` attribute is the index path to one of these objects. The game engine uses fake lights when its artificial intelligence (AI) drives or when other players drive the vehicle in multi-player mode.

✔ `decoration`: Chapter 7 discusses setting proper corona textures for your lights. You get to take advantage of those objects with this attribute. The decoration attribute is the index path to the corona object for your light.

✔ `lightType`: The final attribute for a light on your vehicle is `lightType`. This is a simple integer value that lets the game engine know which light on the vehicle this one is. That way, when the player turns on various lights, the correct ones turn on as expected. This attribute can be set to one of four values:

- 0: Front light
- 1: Back work light
- 2: Front work light
- 3: Headlight

Chapter 12

Defining New Objects and Behaviors with Lua

In This Chapter

▶ Introducing Lua utility functions for GIANTS Engine

▶ Understanding the structure of a mod script

▶ Including custom specializations in your `modDesc.xml` file

*O*ne of the most powerful tools that GIANTS Software has put in the hands of modders is a full-featured application programming interface (API) for its game engine that's accessible via the Lua scripting language. Nearly all the major game functionality for Farming Simulator is written in Lua using this API. You can find 90 percent of the Lua source posted at `www.ls-mods.de/ scriptDocumentation.php`. With these tools in hand, modders have done some incredible things with Farming Simulator and GIANTS Engine. Mods have been as simple as adding the capability for vehicles to have blinking indicator lights to as complex as a flight simulator. With enough time and effort, you can make Farming Simulator do just about anything you can imagine.

To wield this power, familiarize yourself with Lua. As scripting languages go, Lua is very powerful despite its small size and relatively simple syntax. In fact, for this very reason, Lua has become one of the most popular (if not *the* most popular) languages to embed in game engines.

This chapter spells out the very basics of Lua. If you want to know more in-depth information, I suggest that you check out the official Lua website, www.lua.org, You can find information to get started with Lua as well as reference documentation. You can also check out different books. Just go to www.amazon.com and search.

Getting Started with Utils.lua

A mod can take advantage of a package of Lua functions, specific to Farming Simulator. The functions in this package, Utils.lua, are mostly for pulling and identifying data from the various XML files in Farming Simulator and in your mod. Here is a list of each function and what it does:

✔ **Utils.indexToObject()**: Various tags in your vehicle XML file list the index path to a specific object in the Scenegraph. However, your Lua script needs more than the path. It needs the actual object data. In order to get the actual object data into your script, you need this function. You provide a table with all objects and the index path of the one you want. This function returns your object's data.

✔ **Utils.getFilename()**: This constructs a filename that can be used to load resources. In other words, it removes the $ symbol at the beginning of a path and then adds the full path to the mod used by this filename. The second parameter of this function needs to be the base path that you want.

✔ **Utils.getNoNil()**: With this nifty function, you can check a variable for a value. If that value isn't set or doesn't exist, you can choose a default value rather than being stuck with nil.

✔ **Utils.getVectorFromString()**: XML documents are text files. That means that as far as any parser is concerned, the whole thing is just one giant string. There's no differentiation between a string value and a numeric one. So when you pull in a value that's intended to be a vector, such as a set of *x*, *y*, and *z* coordinates, you need to perform a conversion. This function provides that facility.

✔ `Utils.getVectorNFromString()`: Whereas `Utils.getVectorFromString()` returns components to be assigned to individual variables, this function returns the vector in a single table of a size you specify. Do note, however, that if the vector is smaller than the specified table size, this function returns nil for the whole thing.

✔ `Utils.getRadiansFromString()`: In vehicle XML files, angles are written in degrees for human readability. However, in GIANTS Engine (like most game engines), angles are calculated using radians. This utility function converts a string of angles in degrees to a Lua table of angles in radians. Like `Utils.getVectorNFromString()`, you specify the size of the table. If the string has fewer values than fit in the table, the function returns nil.

✔ `Utils.cutFruitArea()`: This function doesn't directly work with data from your vehicle XML file. Instead, it defines an action that your mod (typically a vehicle) does, such as cutting fruit that's reached a minimum growth state. This function doesn't return any values, and the input parameters for it define a parallelogram-shaped area to be cut by your mod.

✔ `Utils.loadParticleSystem()`: Some particle systems in mods are supposed to run all the time, like water through a creek or smoke from a house's chimney. However, some mods require more dynamically activated particle systems, such as seed shooting from a harvester or exhaust from a running tractor. Those particle systems don't run all the time, just when a certain event is triggered. This function loads such a particle system from an XML file.

✔ `Utils.deleteParticleSystem()`: If you can dynamically load a particle system, then you should be able to dynamically remove it as well. That's exactly what this function accomplishes.

✔ **Utils.setEmittingState()**: The Utils. loadParticleSystem() function only loads a particle system into the scene. It doesn't start it or stop it from running. That duty is the designation of this particular function. Using this function, you specify the particle system and whether it's emitting.

You can get a more comprehensive overview of the Utils.lua functions on the script documentation website (www.ls-mods.de/scriptDocumentation. php?class=utils).

Understanding a Specialization Script

If you want your mod to work during multiplayer gameplay, then you have to have at least a basic understanding of how GIANTS Engine's network protocol works. Without doing so, other players won't be able to see the effect of your mod while playing, if they can play at all.

The best way to understand how it works is to have a look at a working script. One of the easiest examples is the honk specialization. A *specialization* in Farming Simulator is a particular feature that vehicle mods can have. A specialization can be a complete set of functionality, such as a sprayer or tractor, or it can be a simple addition, such as saying the vehicle can be filled or have other objects attach to it. Farming Simulator ships with nearly 90 different specializations and any of them are available for use in your own vehicle mods (and with some code and effort, you can even add your own specialization).

One of the default specializations available is the honk specialization. It does exactly what you think. Vehicles with the honk specialization can play a sound when the user activates a honk event. If that event is triggered during multiplayer play, all nearby players also hear the honk sound from that vehicle. GIANTS Engine's network protocol makes it possible. The following is the Lua code for the honk specialization. It's a pretty short file, only 119 lines of code.

```
1    --
2    -- Honk
3    -- Specialization for honking
4    --
5    -- @author  Manuel Leithner
6    -- @date  19/12/2013
7    --
8    -- Copyright (C) GIANTS Software
           GmbH, Confidential, All Rights
           Reserved.
9
10   Honk = {};
11   source("dataS/scripts/vehicles/
           specializations/HonkEvent.
           lua");
12
13   function
14   Honk.prerequisitesPresent
           (specializations)
15      return
16   SpecializationUtil.
           hasSpecialization(Steerable,
           specializations);
17   end;
18
19   function Honk:load(xmlFile)
20
21     self.playHonk = SpecializationUtil.
           callSpecializationsFunction("p
           layHonk");
22
23        if self.isClient then
24            self.sampleHonk = Utils.
           loadSample(xmlFile, {},
           "vehicle.honkSound", nil,
           self.baseDirectory, self.
           components[1].node);
25        end;
26     end;  ·
```

```
27    function Honk:delete()
28       if self.isClient then
29
30          Utils.deleteSample(self.
             sampleHonk);
31       end;
32    end;
33
34    function Honk:readStream(streamId,
          connection)
35    end;
36
37    function Honk:writeStream(streamId,
          connection)
38    end;
39
40    function Honk:mouseEvent(posX, posY,
          isDown, isUp, button)
41    end;
42
43    function Honk:keyEvent(unicode, sym,
          modifier, isDown)
44    end;
45
46    function Honk:update(dt)
47       if self.isEntered and
          self.isClient and
          self:getIsActiveForInput(false)
          then
48       if self.sampleHonk ~= nil then
49          -- only send event if honking
             key is pressed or released
50          if InputBinding.
             isPressed(InputBinding.HONK)
             then
51             if not self.sampleHonk.
                isPlaying then
52
53                self:playHonk(true);
54             end;
55          else
56             if self.sampleHonk.isPlaying
                then
57
58                self:playHonk(false);
```

```
59           end;
60          end;
61        end;
62        end;
63  end;
64
65  function Honk:updateTick(dt)
66  end;
67
68  function Honk:draw()
69  end;
70
71  function Honk:onLeave()
72      Honk.onDeactivateSounds(self);
73  end;
74
75  function Honk:onDetach()
76    Honk.onDeactivateSounds(self);
77  end;
78
79  function Honk:onDeactivateSounds()
80      if self.isClient then
81          Utils.stopSample(self.
            sampleHonk);
82
83            Utils.stop3DSample(self.
              sampleHonk);
84      end;
85  end;
86
87  function Honk:playHonk(isPlaying,
            noEventSend)
88    if self.sampleHonk ~= nil then
89      HonkEvent.sendEvent(self,
            isPlaying, noEventSend);
90
91        if isPlaying then
92            if self:getIsActive() then
93                if
            self:getIsActiveForSound()
            then
94              Utils.playSample(self.
            sampleHonk, 0, 0, nil);
95                elseif self.
            isControlled then
```

```
96                        -- enable 3d
             sound to vehicle on another
             player's game
97                Utils.play3DSample(self.
             sampleHonk);
98                end;
99             end;
100       else
101          Honk.
          onDeactivateSounds(self);
102          end;
103    end;
104  end;
```

The following are the main elements of the script to pay attention to, because they form the basic structure for a specialization script:

✔ **Line 10, Honk = {};:** This is the start of the script. Objects in Lua are based on tables. This line defines the Honk object for GIANTS Engine. It isn't populated yet, but this line serves as a *stub,* or a placeholder.

✔ **Line 11, source();:** The honk script requires an additional script to handle honk events.

✔ **Line 13, function Honk.prerequisites Present():** The honk specialization can only be added to vehicles that also have the steerable specialization. This function verifies that the vehicle trying to honk also has the required steerable specialization.

✔ **Line 17, function Honk:load(xmlFile):** Think of this line as the Honk object's constructor. This function pulls information that's in the vehicle XML file, specifically looking for the honkSound tag and its associated attributes. After this information is loaded, the game engine knows exactly what sound to play and how to play it. This function also dynamically adds an audio source to the scene to play the honk sound, just like you might do in GIANTS Editor.

✔ **Line 41, function Honk:delete():** An object destructor. If the Honk object is no longer needed, this function removes it from memory.

✔ **Line 60,** `function Honk:update(dt):` This function checks for user input. If the honking button is pressed, this function calls `playHonk` (line 99).

✔ **Line 83,** `function Honk:onLeave()` **and line 91,** `function Honk:onDetach():` Both of these functions do exactly the same thing. They disable honk sounds when the player chooses to stop interacting with the vehicle.

✔ **Line 99,** `function Honk:playHonk():` This line is probably the most important function in the script because it actually plays the honk audio both for the player activating the honk as well as other players in a multiplayer game.

Take a closer look at the `Honk:playHonk()` function. In particular, have a look at line 101. It has the following:

```
HonkEvent.sendEvent(self, isPlaying,
        noEventSend);
```

This line of code calls a function from a `HonkEvent` object. Recall that line 11 of this script sources another file. That file is `HonkEvent.lua` and it's there where the magic networking goodness happens. Fortunately, that script is also on the script documentation website and available for you to read. It's even shorter than `Honk.lua`, weighing in at a svelte 49 lines of code:

```
1  -- Copyright (C) GIANTS Software GmbH,
         Confidential, All Rights
         Reserved.
2
3  HonkEvent = {};
4  HonkEvent_mt = Class(HonkEvent,
         Event);
5
6  InitEventClass(HonkEvent,
         "HonkEvent";
7
8  function HonkEvent:emptyNew()
```

```
9        local self =
            Event:new(HonkEvent_mt);
10        return self;
11  end;
12
13  function HonkEvent:new(object,
            isPlaying)
14        local self = HonkEvent:emptyNew()
15        self.object = object;
16      self.isPlaying = isPlaying;
17        return self;
18  end;
19
20  function
            HonkEvent:readStream(streamId,
            connection)
21        local id =
            streamReadInt32(streamId);
22      self.isPlaying =
            streamReadBool(streamId);
23        self.object =
            networkGetObject(id);
24        self:run(connection);
25  end;
26
27  function
            HonkEvent:writeStream(streamId,
            connection)
28        streamWriteInt32(streamId,
            networkGetObjectId(self.
            object));
29      streamWriteBool(streamId, self.
            isPlaying);
30  end;
31
32  function HonkEvent:run(connection)
33        self.object:playHonk(self.
            isPlaying, true);
34        if not connection:getIsServer()
            then
35
            g_server:broadcastEvent(Honk
            Event:new(self.object, self.
```

```
                    isPlaying), nil, connection,
                    self.object);
36      end;
37  end;
38
39  function HonkEvent.sendEvent(vehicle,
            isPlaying, noEventSend)
40      if isPlaying ~= vehicle.
            honkPlaying then
41          if noEventSend == nil or
            noEventSend == false then
42              if g_server ~= nil then
43
            g_server:broadcastEvent(Honk
            Event:new(vehicle, isPlaying),
            nil, nil, vehicle);
44              else
45
            g_client:getServerConnection():
            sendEvent(HonkEvent:new
            (vehicle, isPlaying));
46              end;
47          end;
48      end;
49  end;
```

Quite a bit of this code is boilerplate, meaning you can
make small modifications to it and have a network-
capable event of your own. Here's a quick rundown of the
main functions in this script:

✔ **Line 6, InitEventClass:** This line of code basically registers the honk event with GIANTS Engine,
making the engine aware of the event's existence.
Without this line, you might be able to trigger
events, but the game engine has no idea what they
are or what to do with them.

✔ **Line 13, function HonkEvent:new():** This function creates a new honk event. More importantly, it
prepopulates the event with the honking object to
pay attention to, and the event knows whether it's
already honking.

✔ **Line 20,** `function HonkEvent:readStream()`: Assuming a network connection has been established, this function is how one player's game can check the server to see if another player is honking a horn.

✔ **Line 27,** `function HonkEvent:writeStream()`: The sibling function to `HonkEvent:readStream()`, this one tells the server that a honk is or is not happening.

✔ **Line 32,** `function HonkEvent:run()`: This function is executed when the honk should be enabled. If done at the server, the server sends the event to all players except for the one who initiated the honk.

✔ **Line 39,** `function HonkEvent.sendEvent()`: The `sendEvent()` function is really the workhorse in this script. It verifies that the vehicle is supposed to be playing the sound, ensures that a networking event is supposed to be triggered, and then tells the server to broadcast the event to all players.

Looking at the last function in `HonkEvent.lua`, the work happens in lines 42–45. In line 42, the script checks whether a variable, `g_server`, exists. This is a global variable for GIANTS Engine's Lua API. If this variable exists, then the script knows that the game server is on the current computer. And if that's the case, then this computer is the one that needs to tell the connecting computers, the *clients,* to trigger a honk event. The `g_server:broadcastEvent()` function on line 43 does exactly that.

However, if the current computer isn't running the game server (for example, the `g_server` variable returns nil), then the script knows that it's on a client machine and must therefore connect to the game server and request that a honk event be triggered. To do that, another global variable, `g_client`, is used, as shown in line 45.

Using the information in this chapter along with the official documentation, you could easily override the `honk` specialization with your own. Perhaps instead of just playing a sound when the player presses the honk key, a particle system on the vehicle is enabled. That particle system could sparkle around the vehicle, kind of a visual honk, if you will. Or maybe the particle system simply launches a single potato in the air. Really, the possibilities are limited only by your imagination.

Adding Custom Specializations to `modDesc.xml`

If you've written your own custom specialization in Lua, you need to add an additional block of mark-up to your `modDesc.xml`. (See Chapter 6 for more details on `modDesc.xml`.) You basically need to make GIANTS Engine aware of your script. After you do that, you can treat your custom specialization just like any of the default ones that ship with Farming Simulator.

The additional mark-up that you need belongs within a `specializations` section. Most modders put the `specializations` open and close tags above the `vehicleTypes` tag in their `modDesc.xml`. The mark-up you want to add should look something like this:

```xml
<specializations>
  <specialization name="mySpecialization"
        className="MySpecialization"
        filename="scripts/
        MySpecialization.lua" />
</specializations>
```

The `specialization` tag in the `specializations` section has three attributes:

- ✔ **name:** The custom name you give to your specialization. Anything else that uses this specialization of yours will need to reference this name.

- ✔ **className:** Although this attribute is named the same as that in the `type` tag within the `vehicleTypes` section, its purpose is slightly different. It doesn't refer to a vehicle class. It's a class/object that you've defined in your specialization's Lua file.

✔ **filename:** This attribute should point to the folder that holds your Lua script defining this specialization. Most modders typically have a `scripts` folder within their mod where they place all of the scripts that are relevant to that mod.

After you add this block of mark-up to your `modDesc.xml` file, you can add your specialization within a `type` tag of the `vehicleTypes` section, as I describe in Chapter 6. The total block of mark-up to support your custom specialization would look something like this:

```
<specializations>
  <specialization name="mySpecialization"
          className="MySpecialization"
          filename="scripts/
          MySpecialization.lua" />
</specializations>
<vehicleTypes>
  <type name="myMod" className="Vehicle"
          filename=$dataS/scripts/
          vehicles/Vehicle.lua">
    <specialization
          name="mySpecialization" />
  </type>
</vehicleTypes>
```

Chapter 13

Getting Out Your Mod

• •

In This Chapter

▶ Putting the finishing touches on your mod

▶ Preparing your mod for the in-game store

▶ Letting others play your mod

• •

*Y*ay! Your mod is finished! Now you can share your mod with the world and let other people enjoy using it when they play Farming Simulator.

You may wonder how to get your mod on their computer. Chances are good that you've already installed and played your fair share of other peoples' mods. You at least know how those mods got in your game. You can work that backward to sort out some of the details with just a few finishing touches and polishes that may be somewhat less obvious. This chapter aims to help fill in those blanks.

Finalizing Your Mod

When you first started making your mod, you created a `modDesc.xml` file. More than likely, you only filled in the tags that were really necessary to get your mod working in-game. Perhaps you copied the `modDesc.xml` from the sample mod that comes with Farming Simulator and only made a few minor changes. Now you need to revisit your `modDesc.xml` and make it final.

Here are some important tips to help you finalize your mod. Refer to Chapter 5 for a complete lowdown on setting up your `modDesc.xml` file.

✔ **Author and version:** You want people to know who made this mod, right? Make sure your name is in the author tag. And if you're releasing your mod for the first time and you consider it complete, set the version number to 1.0. Players don't care how many internal versions and revisions you made before release.

✔ **Descriptions:** You can describe your mod in two different places within the `modDesc.xml`: at the beginning for the overall mod and within the `storeItems` tag, for each item in your mod that appears in the in-game store. Make sure these descriptions are up-to-date and accurate.

✔ **Price and upkeep:** Make sure these values are set to realistic numbers before you release.

✔ **Localization:** Because Farming Simulator is a game with an international audience and is played in 12 different languages, you may want to translate the descriptions in your mod to the big three (English, German, French). You can use an online translator to help, but I suggest you find a friend or perhaps someone else in the modding community to help you with any languages you're not familiar with.

✔ **Icons:** The next section of this chapter covers icons in more detail. Just make sure your `modDesc.xml` points to the right files for now.

✔ **Paths to scripts and other assets:** If your mod uses any custom Lua scripts or a customized vehicle XML file, double-check the paths to those files and make sure everything is where it's supposed to be and named appropriately.

I suggest that you also go through the assets in your mod and freshen your naming. Make sure files have names that make sense (for example, `heavyTractor.i3d` instead of `myTest14.i3d`). And check the naming within each file, too. Parts of your mod should be named after what they are or what they do. With releasing a mod comes the implied obligation of maintaining it and fixing any bugs that players discover. Opening an old file of yours to fix a bug and finding the Scenegraph littered with objects that are all named *transform* and *Cube* is a very unpleasant experience. What could have been a 5-minute fix can end up taking much longer because you have to spend time to find that one object in a map, and it has the same generic name as 30 other objects all over the scene.

Creating Store and Brand Icons

How a mod appears in the in-game store can really add to the feeling of completeness. You spent all of this time sweating over every minor detail in creating the 3D assets and scripts for your mod. Don't cheapen it by slapping on a store icon cobbled together in a few minutes in MS Paint.

Furthermore, quite a few mod-hosting sites use the in-game icon as the link to see your mod, so you want to make a good first impression with players who may use your mod. These sections explain how you can wow players with the right store and brand icons.

Editing a store icon

Requirements for the store icon are pretty straightforward — a PNG (or DDS) image that's 256x256 pixels in dimension. In fact, included in Farming Simulator's sdk folder (typically C:\Program Files\Farming Simulator 2015\sdk on a Windows computer) is an image named store_template.png. If you open that file in Photoshop, you can use it as a background for a nice image of your mod.

Personally, I like to render a relatively high-resolution image of the model from my 3D software. However, some people prefer a more in-game look. For that, you can take a screenshot of your mod from within GIANTS Editor. In either case, you can clean and scale that image in Photoshop so it fits in the available space of `store_template.png`.

If you're rendering from a 3D program like Blender, Maya, or 3ds Max, try to render a PNG with an alpha channel for transparency. Doing so can make it easier to overlay on the background of `store_template.png`. You can read more on alpha channels in Chapter 9.

If you're taking a screenshot from within GIANTS Editor, you probably added at least one light so your mod could be seen well. You can hide the lines of that light for a cleaner screenshot by toggling View⇨Show⇨Lights to off in the menu.

After you get your store icon image arranged the way you want, save it as a PNG (or better, a DDS) in your mod's folder. Make sure you use a name that makes sense and double-check that your `modDesc.xml` correctly points to that image.

Adding a brand icon

Whether your mod is a piece of equipment with a known brand or something that you've made on your own, you may want to include an icon for the store that indicates the brand. Brand icons follow the same basic rules as store icons for your mod with only a couple minor differences. Brand icons are PNG or DDS images and have dimensions of 256x128 pixels.

Submitting and Sharing Mods

When you're ready to package and share your mod with the world, these sections can get you up to speed.

Exporting and packaging your mod

When packaging your mod, do a final export from GIANTS Editor into a new folder somewhere else on your hard drive. Doing so can ensure that all of the files required for your mod are in the same place. Doing so is also a quick way to clear out any unnecessary files that may have crept their way into your mod folder. For example, some programs like to leave what I call file litter, which is usually backups of your previously saved version of that file. Blender does this with its .blend1 files, and some text editor programs leave .bak files that serve the same purpose. Exporting leaves those files behind because a player won't need them to run your mod in the game.

To export your mod with all of its necessary files, open it in GIANTS Editor and then take the following steps:

1. **Choose File⇨Export All with Files.**

2. **In the file browser dialog, navigate to the place on your hard drive where you want to export.**

   I like to choose the desktop because it's easy to remember and easy to clean up when I'm done.

3. **Make a new folder for your mod and its files.**

   Depending on your OS, there should be a button in the file browser dialog for making new folders. You also can create a new folder using the right-click menu in the file area.

4. **Type a name for your I3D file.**

   Using the same name you've been using for it is okay.

5. **Repeat the first four steps for each I3D file in your mod.**

6. **After you finish exporting, you may want to double-check your newly exported mod to make sure everything is properly in order and nothing was lost in the process.**

If something is missing, simply copy it over from the original mod folder. For example, scripts may load files that are in none of the I3D files. So be sure to copy any Lua or XML files that you need.

With your mod neatly exported to a fresh new folder, you can package it for sharing with the wider world.

Follow these steps to get your files in a Zip archive in Windows:

1. **From Windows Explorer, go to your export folder and select all files.**

2. **Right-click and choose Send to⇨Compressed (zipped) folder.**

   Depending on the size of your mod, you may have to wait a few seconds after this step while your computer packs all of your files into the Zip. When it's done, you should see a new file sharing the same name as your folder. The only difference is that its icon has a zipper on it. That's your Zip file.

3. **Rename your Zip file to something you like, or you can choose to keep the name as-is and just press Enter on your keyboard.**

Distributing and maintaining your mod

Dozens of sites on the Internet exist with the exclusive purpose of hosting mods for Farming Simulator. Each one has its own mechanism for uploading and approving mods. Because I can't cover them all, decide which site (or sites) you want to use and then read through their guidelines. For this section, I cover the official ModHub on the Farming Simulator website (www.farming-simulator.com/mods.php).

Until recently, the official ModHub was open to submissions by invite only. However, ModHub now accepts submissions from everyone. You just need to set up an account. After you register and log in, you should see a page that looks like Figure 13-1.

Figure 13-1: The default landing page when you first log in to ModHub.

Click on the *Misc* link in ModHub for a guidelines PDF document (in both English and German). Among other things, it gives you a series of short tests you can do on your mod to make sure it's properly formatted and error free.

Stick to these steps for putting your mod on ModHub:

1. Click the Add New button on the main ModHub landing page.

You should see that a new mod has been added, named Untitled Mod. This is the placeholder for your mod. Mods don't show up in the publicly viewable list of mods until they're approved. And in order to get approved, you need to upload your mod and provide some details about it.

2. **Click the mod name and you arrive at a page like the one in Figure 13-2.**

Figure 13-2: After adding a mod placeholder, you can go in and actually upload details on your mod.

This is the ModHub detail page for your mod, and it's ultimately where you upload all of the information pertaining to your mod. Fortunately, because you were so diligent in creating your mod, you should have everything necessary for this page. The following is a short list of what you need:

- **Your mod, packed in a Zip file:** See the previous section about packaging your mod. You have the option here to use the modDesc.xml in your Zip file to fill your mod's *meta data,* or the information about your mod, such as the name, author, and description. Keep this checkbox enabled and many of the other fields of this page should automatically populate.

- **Mod icons:** ModHub gives you the ability to upload two different sizes of icons for listing on the site. You can just upload the store icon you created for your mod for both, and the site will automatically scale it to fit.

- **Localized title and description:** If you chose to load meta data from your `modDesc`. `xml`, these fields should already be filled in. Otherwise, you can fill them in manually.

- **Categories:** Categories aren't part of the `modDesc.xml`, so you need to make some decisions here. You can add your mod into up to three different categories. Make sure the categories you choose are appropriate in order to help people find your mod.

- **Screenshot:** This is typically an image of your mod taken from within Farming Simulator. The preferred size for this image is 560x350 pixels. Fortunately, the ModHub uploader automatically scales your image for you if you want.

3. **Make sure all of the fields are properly filled in, and you're good to go.**

4. **Submit your mod for certification by clicking the Submit button at the top of your mod's ModHub detail page and waiting for it to be approved.**

The approval process may take a day or two.

You've created a mod and you're releasing it to the world. This mod is your responsibility. Players expect that if they run into a problem with your mod or if they have a question about it, you can fix the problem or try to answer the question. Most sites that host mods give you the ability to upload updates and fixes to your mod. Take advantage of this feature. Doing so makes you a positive contributor to the Farming Simulator community and the modding community in general. Maintain your first mod well and you'll have a group of players eager to try out your next one when it's ready.

A note on copyright and trademark

Copyrights and trademarks aren't the same. *Copyright* protects a thought or idea expressed in a fixed medium, such as writing, a picture, or sound. *Trademark,* on the other hand, is a bit more nebulous. It's about defining how a business is identified in the world, its brand. An organization can trademark all kinds of things, pictures, words, sounds, and even smells! For example, a famous motorcycle company has trademarked the sound of one of its engines because people hear that sound and associate it with that company.

Laws about each vary a tad from country to country, but generally speaking, a major difference between the two is that in the case of a trademark, the owner of the mark is legally obligated to contact anyone who infringes on it and insist that the person or organization stops. If the trademark owner doesn't do so, they risk losing their trademark. Copyright has no such requirement.

You could possibly include something in your mod that is perfectly acceptable in terms of copyright, but still has the potential to get you a cease and desist letter for a trademark violation. Although the chances are pretty slim, you should still be aware of the possibility.

Part V
The Part of Tens

In this part . . .

- ✔ Examine additional available online resources to help take your modding to the next level
- ✔ Troubleshoot problems by using different available resources from the Farming Simulator community
- ✔ Discover how to avoid common pitfalls and frustration when creating your mods

Chapter 14

Ten Powerful Tips When Creating Mods

● ●

In This Chapter

▶ Utilizing correct image formats

▶ Naming filenames correctly

▶ Referencing the game log

● ●

*W*hen making your mods, you more than likely will run into a number of issues repeatedly. Think of this chapter as a checklist you can go over if your mod isn't performing as well as you think it should.

Use the Correct Image Format for Textures

GIANTS Engine supports the very common PNG image format. However, PNG images aren't optimized for use in real-time game graphics, so your mod will load slower and perform more poorly if you use PNG images. The recommended format to use is the DirectDraw Surface (DDS) format. You can find details for converting PNG files to DDS files in Chapter 9.

Use Texture Sizes that Fit Your Mod's Physical Size

When creating mods, make sure that the texture sizes that you use are appropriate for the size of your mod. Say, for the sake of argument, that you create a simple mod with a pebble on the game map. That pebble is never going to be more than a handful of pixels on-screen. So using a gigantic 2k texture doesn't make a lot of sense. Use something much smaller so the game engine doesn't spend a lot of time loading texture data that the player is never going to be able to appreciate.

On the other hand, if your mod is a large tractor, use a suitably sized texture for it. A 16x16 pixel texture would look horrible on a model that large.

Consolidate Your Texture Data

Optimizing for performance is full of trade-offs. If you have a lot of small textures, then GIANTS Engine spends a lot of time pulling those images from your hard drive and loading them into memory. However, you can reduce that load time if you group all of your texture data into a few large images that the engine only has to load once. (The previous two sections help the textures load fast.) Consolidating texture data complicates UV unwrapping (see Chapter 7) a bit, but the performance benefits are worth the effort.

Set Useful Clip Distance Values

The *clip distance* attributes relate to the virtual cameras in GIANTS Engine. They're used for making objects invisible in the distance. You should use values as small as possible. The values you choose are mostly dependent on the size of the object, its importance, and the construction. For example, a tractor's body most likely hides a steering wheel, so the clip distance for the steering wheel can be smaller.

Avoid Spaces and Special Characters in Filenames

You may find yourself in a situation where a texture doesn't appear on a 3D model or a script doesn't load or your mod doesn't work altogether. This problem often is a result of giving your files and assets poor names. Generally speaking, avoid using spaces and other special characters such as the ampersand (&) and the "at" symbol (@) in your filenames. You should also avoid using characters with diacritical marks like accents and umlauts.

Be Aware of Case-Sensitive Paths

Stay aware of case-sensitive paths if you want to guarantee that your mod works on every operating system that can run Farming Simulator. In Windows, it doesn't matter whether a letter in a file path is uppercase or lowercase. However, on most other operating systems, such as Mac OS X and Linux, it *does* matter. On those machines, a lowercase *f* is very different from an uppercase *F*.

Because of that sensitivity to case, you should pay close attention to whether a letter is uppercase or lowercase when referencing a file path from XML or a Lua script. Use *camel case* when naming (just imagine a camel's hump). That is, the first word in a filename is all lowercase and the first letter of each subsequent word is uppercase with no spaces between words. For example, if you want to call your mod "Best Mod Ever," then your mod's folder name should look like this: `bestModEver`. Every time you reference your mod's folder, use that exact spelling and capitalization.

Convert WAV Files from Stereo to Mono

GIANTS Engine supports 3D sound, meaning that if you have a cow to your left, the game engine is smart enough to send that cow's sound only to the left speaker. Because the game engine handles determining which speaker gets sound, the sounds in your mod should be in mono. Stereo sound files just give the engine unnecessary work and wastes hard drive space.

So if you have any 3D or stereo sounds in your mod, mix them down to mono.

Check the Game Log for Errors and Warnings

Sometimes you'll release a mod that appears to work well in-game when you test it. However, you may overlook a missing file, a texture may be in PNG instead of DDS, or an audio file in stereo that should be in mono. The log gives useful warning messages, many of which are covered in Appendix A. If you pay attention, you avoid bug reports after you release and you can also get hints as to what parts of your mod could be optimized for better performance.

Test Your Mod in Single and Multiplayer Modes

I can't emphasize enough that you test your mod thoroughly in as many different scenarios as you can imagine. Gamers are good at finding new and interesting ways to break games, including your mod.

A modder can often forget about testing in multiplayer mode. You can get so wrapped up in your single player tests that you overlook multiplayer. The next thing you know, you get an email from another player letting you know that the blinking lights on your vehicle don't blink at all in multiplayer mode or that you have a particle system that isn't synchronized across all users.

Put Your Mod into a Single Zip Package

Nothing is more frustrating for a user than going through a complex series of steps just to get a mod working in a game. Complex installation procedures are annoying, and they're a quick way to alienate people. You want to make it easy for others to use your mod, so take the complexity out of it for them.

Most players of Farming Simulator are already quite comfortable and familiar with installing mods from Zip files. Cater to what they're used to.

Chapter 15

Ten Valuable Community Resources

In This Chapter

▶ Using the different Farming Simulator online websites

▶ Turning to other modders for tips and help

*F*arming Simulator emphasizes the value of collaboration. This mindset is extended to and, really, exemplified by the Farming Simulator modding community. This huge community is extremely interested in helping you make your mods. In fact, literally dozens of websites are dedicated to Farming Simulator mods. This chapter mentions ten of the best ones for getting you started.

GIANTS Developer Network

The GIANTS Developer Network (GDN) — located at http://gdn.giants-software.com — is the "Home of the GIANTS Engine." Not only is this site the best place to download the latest exporter plugins for Blender, Maya, and 3ds Max, as well as updates to GIANTS Editor, but it also includes a plethora of useful technical documentation and community forums for interacting with other modders. This site is the best way to provide feedback and report bugs to developers at GIANTS Software.

Modhub

Modhub (`www.farming-simulator.com/mods.php`) is the official repository of Farming Simulator mods. You can find it right on the Farming Simulator website with official mods from GIANTS Software as well as community-contributed mods. Perhaps your mod can be there as well!

Farming Simulator Forums

These forums (`http://forum.giants-software.com`) are the general forums for Farming Simulator. You can find a specific subforum for modding, but you also should pay attention to the other subforums. They're a great place for getting ideas about the types of mods in which players are interested.

Farming Simulator Modding Video Tutorials

This site (`http://gdn.giants-software.com/videoTutorials.php`) is a downloadable content (DLC) package that is bundled with Farming Simulator 2015. It's an excellent series of video tutorials that can help you get started with modding. It is also available on Steam.

Farming Simulator Script Source Code

The best way to get into scripting for Farming Simulator mods is to look at working examples. This site (`www.ls-mods.de/scriptDocumentation.php`) is the place to go. You can find a basic overview of the scripting classes and a large set of examples that you can pore over to see how they work.

GIANTS Software Company Website

For the latest news about upcoming Farming Simulator releases and a general understanding of what is going on with GIANTS Software, there's no better place than the official company website (www.giants-software. com). You can also see the other games that are being released if reading this book has sparked your interest in making mods for those games, too!

Lua.org

This is the official website (www.lua.org) for the Lua scripting language. If you need to get yourself up to speed with your general knowledge on Lua, you can't find a better place to start. Chapter 12 discusses some basics of Lua.

Freesound.org

A mod can be pretty boring and empty without good sound to accompany it. This website (www.freesound. org) hosts a gigantic database of sounds that are available under a Creative Commons license. And if you record or create your own sounds, this site is also a great place to share them with others.

Blender.org

Blender is an incredibly powerful 3D content creation suite that also happens to be free and open source. That means you can download it for free from www.blender.org and use it to make the 3D models in your mod. This site is also a gateway to documentation on Blender as well as its incredibly helpful user community.

CGTextures.com

This website (www.cgtextures.com) features an enormous repository of textures that you can use to add realism to your 3D models.

Make sure that you pay close attention to the licensing information and FAQ on the site. There are a few restrictions on how you may use these textures.

Appendix

Error and Warning Message Reference

● ●

*R*unning into errors isn't uncommon when working with mods. A file may be missing or misnamed. A sound will be in stereo and not mono. A texture will be in PNG format instead of DDS. Some of these problems only cause a minor bump in performance or prevent part of your mod from appearing in-game. Others can cause the game to crash. GIANTS Engine spits out errors and warnings to the game log. This appendix gives a rundown of the possible warnings and errors you may see so you can track down the related issues and squash them before you release your mod to the general public.

General

These types of general error messages point out problems with loading files in the engine:

> ✔ **Error: Could not init 3D system. Shader Model 3.0 is required. Please install the latest video drivers.** This message means that either your video card can't run Farming Simulator or your video card drivers for your operating system aren't up-to-date enough to run Farming Simulator. You can try updating your drivers, but if they're already updated, you may need to investigate getting a new video card.

> ✔ **Error: CRC64 files check failed. Data files are changed. Please reinstall application. Continue anyway?** If you get this error, it means that a vital

file in GIANTS Engine has been corrupted some-how, and the only way to fix it is to replace the file. Because you can't be sure which file is the offending one, the recommendation is to reinstall the game.

✔ **Warning: Character *X* not found in texture font (*myString*).** Farming Simulator ships with a fixed set of characters it can display. If you have a string that uses a character that isn't available, you'll get this warning.

XML Loading

The following errors specifically pertain to loading XML files, such as the vehicle XML file:

✔ **Error: Parse error in *fileName* (*lineNumber*): *parseErrorDescription*.** When GIANTS Engine is parsing (reading) an XML file, it may come to part of the file that is improperly formatted and give you this error. You get rid of this error by going to the line of the problematic file and fixing it.

✔ **Warning: Deleting object '*objectName*' before all triggers are removed.** A script object can dynami-cally create triggers. You run into this warning if your script deletes an object with triggers. The warn-ing message is meant to remind you to delete the triggers first, and *then* delete the object.

✔ **Warning: Ignoring multiple overlay changes within one frame for '*objectName*'.** If you change the UVs of an overlay multiple times within the space of a single frame of animation, you'll see this warning message. This is because of how GIANTS Engine stores overlay objects. It can't render them twice with different UVs in the course of a single frame.

✔ **Mac case sensitivity check.** This warning is only pres-ent on Windows computers. Because the Windows file system isn't case-sensitive, the system has addi-tional precautions to help ensure your mod works in Mac OS X and Linux as well as it does in Windows.

> 🖊 **Warning: Loading file with invalid case:** *fileName.*
> You get this warning on Windows when you have
> a filename stipulated in your XML one way, but it's
> capitalized differently in the file's actual name.

Script

You may get one of these errors when working with
custom scripts:

> 🖊 **Error: LUA running function '*methodName*'.** If you
> have a Lua script and it fails while running a specific
> method, this error message is intended to help you
> find the offending method so you can fix it.

> 🖊 **Error: getChildAt index out of range.** The
> getChildAt() function takes an integer value as
> a parameter. If that number is larger than the array
> of children for a given object, you'll get this error. It
> usually means your object doesn't have the number
> of children you expect it to have in your script.

Overlays

If your mod incorporates a video overlay, then you may
run into the following error:

> 🖊 **Error: VideoOverlay, width or height doesn't equal
> 2^n.** Video overlays need to be of specific dimensions.
> Both the height and the width of the video need to be a
> number that's a power of two. Otherwise, it won't play.

Joints

If your mod incorporates joints, such as those used in
some vehicles, then you may see these errors:

> 🖊 **Error: setJointFrame, actor must be 0 or 1.** Your
> script is trying to set up an invalid joint. The second
> parameter of the setJointFrame() function is the

`actor` parameter, and you must set it to either 0 or 1 in your script. Either you've forgotten to include this parameter or your script is trying to set it to be something other than a 0 or 1.

✔ **Error: Invalid joint index *indexNumber*.** This error means the number of IK joints is lower than the engine expects. You run into this error when using the `setJointTransformGroup()` function.

✔ **Error: Invalid joint transform group id *idNumber*.** IK joints can be assigned to transform groups in Lua scripts. However, if you try to assign a joint to a transform group that GIANTS Engine isn't aware of (either because it isn't there or because you're using the wrong ID number), you'll get this error.

✔ **Error: setScale, scale is not allowed for dynamic objects.** Dynamic objects can't be scaled. If you try to scale a dynamic object from your script, you'll get this error.

I3D Loading

Although the I3D format is based on XML, GIANTS Engine provides the following messages specifically when loading faulty I3D files:

✔ **Error: Can't load resource: *resourceName*.** Your I3D file references an asset (object, texture, sound, and so on) that doesn't appear to exist or is named differently than the game engine expects.

✔ **Error: Incorrect I3D version. Version 1.6 required. File *fileName*.** You usually run into this error when you've exported a model from Blender, Maya, or 3ds Max with an older exporter. Use a more up-to-date exporter to export your object to fix this error.

✔ **Error: Parse error in *fileName* at line *lineNumber*.** You get this error when something is poorly formatted with your I3D file. Fortunately, this message gives you the line number where it thinks the error occurs, so you can open the file in a text editor like Notepad++ and try to resolve the issue.

✔ **Error: Too many custom maps! Maximal 6 allowed.** GIANTS Engine has a limit on the total number of custom textures you can use per material. You'll need to find a way to reduce or consolidate your textures.

✔ **Error: Too many custom parameters! Maximal 10 allowed.** GIANTS Engine has a limit on the number of custom parameters that you can use per material. You'll need to find a way to reduce how many you're using.

✔ **Error: Failed to load terrain detail layer** *layerName.* This error means that the density file of the terrain's detail layer wasn't found or some other parameters are wrong.

✔ **Error: Failed to load terrain foliage layer** *layer-Name.* This error means that the density file of the terrain's detail layer wasn't found or some other parameters are wrong.

✔ **Error:** *terrainName* **distance texture** *'fileName'* **not found.** The texture that you've defined as the *distance texture* for level of detail (LOD) purposes isn't where GIANTS Engine expects it to be, or that file is named differently than it expects.

✔ **Error:** *terrainName* **distance texture** *'fileName'* **incorrect format. Must be 8bit RGB format.** 8-bit RGB images are the most common. But sometimes, you may accidentally use a grayscale image or a high bit-depth image (such as 16-bit) or even an image with an indexed palette. None of those image types will work in GIANTS Engine. You need to convert the image to 8-bit RGB.

✔ **Error: Shape (***shapeSize***B) in** *'fileName'* **too big. Maximum supported is 4194304B.** GIANTS Engine can't load a single file that's larger than 4MB in size. If you get this error, you'll need to find a way to reduce the size of your geometry. Usually that means reducing the amount of vertices and triangles used to construct a mesh.

✔ **Error: Traffic system road spline '*splineName*' dead-end at *xCoordinate yCoordinate*.** Splines intended to control traffic need to be *cyclic,* or closed loops. This error means that the spline in question is still open. The error message is even nice enough to let you know, with coordinates in 3D space, where the spline isn't closed.

✔ **Error: Mesh '*meshName*' has zero triangles.** This message means you have what's known as an empty object. The object container exists, but no mesh data is inside. If you exported your scene from Blender, you can sometimes see it if you've deleted all of a mesh's vertices in Edit mode, but never deleted the object from Object mode. Delete it and this error should disappear.

✔ **Error: Emitter shape not found in particle system '*particleSystemName*'.** GIANTS Engine can't find the object that's supposed to be emitting your particles. That object may have been accidentally deleted or the shape id is wrong because references are made by internal id.

✔ **Error: Material not found in particle system '*particleSystemName*'.** GIANTS Engine can't find the material that defines the look of your particle system. Perhaps the material no longer exists or the material id is incorrect.

✔ **Error: ParticleSystem does not support 32bit emitter meshes '*particleSystemName*'.** The referenced emitter shape has more than 65,535 vertices. You need to reduce the number of vertices in your emitter.

✔ **Error: UVs out of range [-8,8] *meshName*.** GIANTS Engine converts a mesh's UVs from floating point values to *short* integer values for optimal performance on video cards. If any of your UV coordinates are in a position that's less than -8 or greater than 8, you'll get this error. To fix, adjust your UVs in Blender, Maya, or 3ds Max, and re-export.

✓ **Error: Failed to create compound** *transformGroup-Name* **with** *numberOfChildren* **children. Maximum is 32.** A compound transform group can only have up to 32 members (children). Consolidate objects or simply reduce the number of compound children in the group.

✓ **Error: Unsupported 32bit index mesh cooking:** *transformGroupName.* The referenced collision object has more than 65,535 vertices. You need to reduce the number of vertices in your collision object.

✓ **Warning: 3D stereo sound files are not supported. Convert** *'soundFile'* **to mono.** GIANTS Engine has detected that you're using a stereo sound file. It prefers sound files to be mono. You can easily fix this by opening the WAV file in a sound editing program like Audacity, mixing down the audio into a single channel, and exporting it. Chapter 10 has more on this process.

✓ **Warning: Shape** *transformGroupName* **(idNumber) not found. Replaced with empty transform group.** Either a transform group has been accidentally deleted from the file or it has a different shape id than the engine expects. GIANTS Engine tries to fix the issue by making an empty transform group. That means the mod will still run, but the problem isn't solved. Objects will be missing from your mod when you look for them in Farming Simulator.

✓ **Warning: Material with id** *idNumber* **not found in shape** *'shapeName'.* This message can happen when you have a material id defined for a shape, but it doesn't exist in the I3D file. GIANTS Engine can't find the material for that shape. You typically get this error if you've manually edited the XML or the I3D file by hand.

✔ **Warning: AudioSource** *audioSourceFile.wav* **file not found.** GIANTS Engine can't find an audio source file that's supposed to be triggered somewhere in your mod. A file-naming issue can usually cause it, but the warning can also crop up if you've deleted the audio source file.

✔ **Warning: Max bones per skinned mesh limit exceeded.** For optimal GPU performance, GIANTS Engine has a limit on the number of bones you can use for deforming meshes. In this case, the mod will still run, but parts of your animation may not move like you expect. To fix, simplify your animation rig.

✔ **Error: Can't add keyframe. Time is not strictly monotonic increasing.**

✔ **Error: Can't add keyframe. Keyframe controls not the same attributes.**

✔ **Warning (compatibility): Texture** *textureFileName* **width or height doesn't equal 2^n.** The 13D format supports using textures of any arbitrary size. However, as noted in Chapter 9, GIANTS Engine needs the width and height of texture images to be a power of two. Your 13D file will import, but for your textures to show up properly in the engine, you need to adjust in Blender, Maya, or 3ds Max, and re-export.

✔ **Warning (performance): Texture** *textureFileName* **raw format.** The texture referenced by your 13D file is in an uncompressed format such as a 24-bit RGB or 32-bit RGBA file. The 13D file will import, but using this texture will hurt game performance. The fix would be to open the texture in Photoshop and save it as a DDS file, as Chapter 9 discusses.

Terrain

On map-related mods, you can get the following errors pertaining to the map's terrain:

📏 **Error: Failed to load height map '*fileName*'.** The image file that defines your terrain's height map is either missing or named differently than the engine expects it to be.

📏 **Error: Load height map '*fileName*': height and width must be equal.** Height maps for terrain must be square images. If your image is rectangular (even a little), then you'll get this error.

📏 **Error: Load height map '*fileName*': width must either be n^2 or n^2+1.** Like with video overlays, the dimensions of a height map have constraints. In the case of height maps, the width of the image must be a power of two (such as 1024) or a 1 plus a power of two (for example, 1025). And because height maps need to be square, the dimension constraint on width also goes for the image's height.

📏 **Error: Terrain layer texture '*fileName*' not found.** The image file that defines your terrain's texture is either missing or named differently than how the engine expects.

📏 **Error: Terrain weight map '*fileName*' not found.** The image file that defines your terrain's weight map is either missing or named differently than how the engine expects.

📏 **Error: Terrain weight map '*fileName*' incorrect format. Must be 8bit single channel.** An 8-bit single channel image is a grayscale image. Unlike regular image textures (which should be 8-bit RGB images), the weight map texture needs to be grayscale. You can make this conversion in Photoshop.

📏 **Error: Terrain weight map '*fileName*' size incorrect. Same size as is needed.** Like height maps, weight maps must be square images. No rectangles.

✔ **Error: Failed to load layer texture *'fileName'* to calculate distance color.** This image file is either missing or named differently than what the engine expects. The image file could also be corrupt and can't be loaded.

✔ **Error: Global layer map *'fileName'* does not have 3 channels.** A layer map image should be an RGB image. If the image is grayscale, then it only has one channel (which isn't enough). If the image is RGBA with an alpha channel, then it has four channels, which is too many. Do the necessary conversions in Photoshop to make your layer map image a nice, three-channel RGB image.

Textures

Most mods involve textures, so there is a high likelihood that you may see one of these error messages:

✔ **Error: Texture, invalid texture type *(textureName)*.** GIANTS Engine doesn't support 3D textures, only 2D and cube textures.

✔ **Error: Texture, width or height too big.** Image textures can be no wider or taller than 2048 pixels. If your image texture exceeds that limit, you'll get this error.

✔ **Error: Texture, width or height doesn't equal 2^n.** The width and height of image textures must be a power of two. See Chapter 9 for more on proper texture sizing.

✔ **Error: DXT Texture, width or height doesn't equal 4*n.** A DXT texture is a GPU-compressed format that comes in DDS files. GIANTS Engine supports DXT1, DXT3, and DXT5. In this error, the width and height of a DXT texture must be a multiple of four (4, 8, 12, 16, and so on). Break out your calculator and scale or crop your image accordingly.

🖊 **Error: Foliage, not enough channels to store states.**
This error occurs when your foliage system uses more
states (bit channels) than the supplied binary data
files have to store them. This error often happens if
the foliage setup in the I3D file has been changed by
hand without updating the binary files to support
more bit channels.

Foliage

A map mod typically has foliage (this is Farming Simulator,
after all). So if you're creating a map mod, you may run
into one of these messages:

🖊 **Warning: Deprecated I3D foliage feature 'has-
GrowthAtlas'. Use 'texCoords' instead.** You typically
run into this error if your mod was created with an
older version of GIANTS Engine. Follow the advice of
the warning and it should go away.

🖊 **Warning: Deprecated I3D foliage feature 'showFirst-
GrowthState'. Use 'texCoords' instead.** You typically
run into this error if your mod was created with an
older version of GIANTS Engine. Follow the advice of
the warning and it should go away.

🖊 **Warning: Deprecated I3D terrain detail feature
'densityMapShaderName'. Use 'densityMapShader
Names' instead.** You typically run into this error
if your mod was created with an older version of
GIANTS Engine. Follow the advice of the warning
and it should go away.

🖊 **Warning: Deprecated I3D foliage feature 'distance-
Colors'. Use 'distanceMapIds' and 'distanceMap
UnitSizes' instead.** You typically run into this error
if your mod was created with an older version of
GIANTS Engine. Follow the advice of the warning
and it should go away.

✔ Warning: Deprecated I3D terrain detail feature 'combinedValuesNumChannels'. Use 'combined-ValuesChannels' instead. You typically run into this error if your mod was created with an older version of GIANTS Engine. Follow the advice of the warning and it should go away.

✔ Warning: No texture repetition supported for block meshes, in foliage '*foliageName*'. Foliage block meshes must have UVs with values in the range between 0 and 1.

✔ Warning: Combined values channels are out of range in '*foliageName*'. The combined values channels must be equal to or lower than the number of density map channels.

✔ Warning: Distance color with a bigger LOD texture than the density map are not supported yet. Distance color textures must be smaller or equal in size to the density map.

Custom shader

If you're using a custom shader in your mod, then you may run into one of the following messages:

✔ Error: Out-dated custom shader. '*fileName*' has version *versionNumber*. Please convert this file to version 2. You typically run into this error if your mod was created with an older version of the GIANTS SDK. Update your custom shader so it follows the SDK version stipulated in the error.

✔ Error: CustomShader, LOD distances have to be sorted. The LOD nodes in a custom shader must be ordered such that their Start Distance attributes are monotonically increasing.

✔ Warning: Deprecated LOD textures/parameters in '*fileName*'. A custom shader should define its textures and parameters in the root node of the XML file instead of inside the LodLevel nodes.

FBX Import

FBX support in GIANTS Engine is a relatively new thing. Although the engine supports FBX well, you may have problems with some exported files, such as the following warning messages:

✓ **Warning: Unsupported light type.** GIANTS Engine doesn't support all of the different types of lights that are available in the FBX format. Only point, spot, and directional lights are supported. If your FBX file uses a light other than those three, the engine will simply use a default light in its place. Of course, you can get rid of the warning by only using the types of lights supported by GIANTS Engine.

✓ **Warning: Unsupported spline format periodic.** GIANTS Engine only supports closed and open splines. If your FBX file has a periodic spline, you'll see this warning. This message won't stop your file from importing, but if you're counting on using a periodic spline, the results won't be as you expect.

Index

Notes

Notes

About the Author

Jason van Gumster is an animator, educator, and entre-
preneur responsible for animations and visual effects for
television, film, and video games. His fascination with the
creative, technical, and business challenges associated
with collaborative productions has allowed him to
manage large international production teams on ridicu-
lously tight deadlines (4 to 7 minutes of animation in just
two days) . . . for fun. A big proponent of open source software, Jason uses open source tools where ever possible.
Author of *Blender For Dummies* (and co-author of *GIMP
Bible*), he is heavily involved in the Blender community.
He's an administrator on the largest Blender user forum
and a member of the Blender Certification Review Board.

Currently based just outside of Atlanta, Georgia, Jason
spends the majority of his time drinking coffee and trying
to be awesome. Hopefully every now and again, he suc-
ceeds at the latter.

Christian Ammann is co-founder and CEO of GIANTS
Software. He holds a master's in computer science from
the University of Berne in Switzerland.

Before founding GIANTS Software in 2006, he gained experience in the game industry at Sony Computer Entertainment
and NVIDIA.

Dedication

To my wife and sons. Thanks for tolerating the long nights
and missed weekends.

Author Acknowledgments

Of course, the biggest thanks goes to GIANTS Software.
Not only have they produced an immensely enjoyable
game in Farming Simulator, but they've also made it incredibly accessible to modders. Their foresight in design and

openness with their tools stands as an example of "doing it right." And the insight they provided on technical matters was immensely valuable in ensuring the book's accuracy.

Just as important, I need to acknowledge the team that brought this book to life, especially Kyle Looper and Chad Sievers at John Wiley & Sons, Inc. Without Kyle, this book wouldn't exist at all. Without Chad, my ham-fisted attempts at wielding the English language would be revealed for what they really are.

And to close, I must not only thank my wife and sons, but applaud them. Their patience for my sleep deprivation and tolerance for my absent-mindedness while writing this book are beyond compare. Thank you, thank you, thank you. You're the best.

Publisher's Acknowledgments

For general information on our other products and services, or how to create a custom *For Dummies* book for your business or organization, please contact our Business Development Department in the U.S. at 877-409-4177, contact info@dummies.biz, or visit www.wiley.com/go/custompub. Some of the people who helped bring this book to market include the following:

Development Editor and Project Editor: Chad R. Sievers

Acquisitions Editor: Kyle Looper

Editorial Manager: Rev Mengle

Brand Licensing Manager: Ali DellaPenna

Custom Publishing Project Specialist: Michael Sullivan

Cover photo: Courtesy of GIANTS Software

Dummies Marketing: Jen Webb

Project Coordinator: Melissa Cossell